THE **PROOF**
ABOUT **ISRAEL**

C.W. Steinle

The Proof about Israel

Prophecy and the Modern State of Israel

C. W. Steinle

2026

The Proof about Israel

Prophecy and the Modern State of Israel

By C. W. Steinle

Copyright © 2026 by Memorial Crown Press
Phoenix, AZ, USA

ISBN: 979-8-9919337-6-6

Note: This manuscript does not consistently quote from a single Bible translation. It uses a mixed-text tradition, drawing primarily from KJV / NKJV, with several passages clearly reflecting ESV / NASB-style modernization. Scripture quotations marked (KJV) are from the King James Version of the Bible, which is in the public domain. Scripture quotations marked (NKJV) are taken from the New King James Version®. Copyright © 1982 by Thomas Nelson. Used by permission. All rights reserved. Scripture quotations marked (ESV) are from the ESV® Bible (The Holy Bible, English Standard Version®), copyright © 2001 by Crossway, a publishing ministry of Good News Publishers. Used by permission. All rights reserved. Scripture quotations marked (NASB) are taken from the (NASB®) New American Standard Bible®, Copyright © 1960, 1971, 1977, 1995, 2020 by The Lockman Foundation. Used by permission. All rights reserved. www.lockman.org.

About the Author

C. W. Steinle is a Christian author and teacher whose work bridges faith, history, and science. With more than twenty-five books to his name, he is known for challenging popular assumptions about prophecy while opening new vistas for Christian thought. Steinle has taught on location in Israel, Greece, and Egypt, blending scholarship with experience. He lives in Phoenix, Arizona, with his wife, Gwen, where they share a passion for biblical studies and family life.

Contents

Preface

Israel is one of the few subjects capable of igniting a room instantly—whether the room is a church fellowship hall, a university classroom, or a livestream chat. In recent years, that heat has only intensified. Prophecy teaching has increasingly been shaped by immediacy. News headlines are read alongside prophetic texts, and interpretive conclusions are drawn.

High-profile commentators speak about Israel with confidence, often in explicitly biblical terms, while activist movements speak with equal certainty in moral and political terms. Both sides can sound absolute. Yet beneath the soundbites is a quieter reality: many Christians who share the same Bible do not share the same prophetic assumptions. That difference matters more than most people realize.

For some believers, the modern State of Israel is essentially unrelated to prophecy—an important nation, a meaningful story, but not an end-times sign. For others, Israel's rebirth in 1948 is treated as a prophetic milestone that "starts the clock" of end-time events.

In that framework, headlines become interpretive keys, and world events are read as direct fulfillments. The result has been a long trail of confident timetables—each one eventually revised, replaced, or quietly forgotten.

The Bible speaks often and powerfully about Israel. It does so in historical terms, covenantal terms, prophetic terms, and eschatological terms. To treat Israel as irrelevant to Scripture is therefore impossible. But to treat modern Israel as *self-evidently identical* to the prophetic Israel of Scripture is equally careless. The question is not whether Israel matters. The question is **how** Israel matters—and **according to which criteria**.

CONTEMPORARY INFLUENCERS AND FRACTURED CONSENSUS

One of the most striking features of the present debate over Israel is not merely its intensity, but the way it has fractured along unexpected ideological lines. For much of the late twentieth and early twenty-first centuries, support for Israel—particularly among American conservatives and evangelical Christians—functioned axiomatically as a given. That assumption has now collapsed. In its place stands a polarized and public dispute among cultural, political, and media influencers whose platforms reach tens of millions. Their diametric positions mirror closely the interpretive categories examined throughout this book.

Tucker Carlson

On one end of the spectrum are figures who frame modern Israel as a moral liability, a destabilizing foreign entanglement, or even a malign influence on American life. Media personality Tucker Carlson has become emblematic of this shift. In a widely circulated post questioning American military and diplomatic support, Carlson asked bluntly, "Why are we defending mass murder in Gaza? Because our greatest ally demands it. It's time to rethink that relationship."[1] The statement is not merely critical of Israeli policy; it implies a coercive dynamic in which American moral judgment is overridden by allegiance to Israel.

Carlson has repeatedly pressed this theme in interviews, arguing that the United States has "no overriding strategic interest" in Israel and describing

---

[1] Tucker Carlson, X (formerly Twitter), December 11, 2025.

the relationship as a "net burden."[2] In another context, he questioned whether Israel's military actions against Christian sites and populations are accidental at all, asking, "Why are American Christians supporting Israeli persecution of Christians?"[3] Such remarks place Israel not within a biblical narrative of restoration, but within a geopolitical framework of suspicion, power imbalance, and moral compromise.

Candace Owens

This skepticism has been echoed—and radicalized—by other influential voices. Candace Owens, for example, has advanced a far more conspiratorial interpretation, repeatedly alleging that Israeli or "Zionist" interests exert hidden control over American politics, media, and conservative institutions. In one post she wrote, "Remember, if they aren't lying they aren't breathing," referring to Israel and its defenders.[4] Elsewhere she accused

---

[2] Tucker Carlson, interview at the Doha Forum, December 2025.

[3] Tucker Carlson, interview discussing Christian populations and Israeli policy, August 2025.

[4] Candace Owens, X (formerly Twitter), September 17, 2025.

Israel of blackmailing U.S. leaders and manipulating public narratives through donor pressure and intelligence operations.[5] These claims move well beyond policy critique into the realm of civilizational antagonism, portraying Israel not merely as flawed, but as fundamentally deceptive and hostile.

What is noteworthy is not only the content of these accusations, but their reception. Such claims—once relegated to fringe discourse—now circulate openly within mainstream conservative and populist media ecosystems, drawing both applause and condemnation. The result is a public rupture in what was once assumed to be a unified pro-Israel front.

Ben Shapiro

Opposing this trend are equally prominent figures who defend Israel's legitimacy, military actions, and strategic necessity with equal force. Ben Shapiro has emerged as one of the most consistent and articulate voices in this camp. In response to accusations of genocide or apartheid, Shapiro has framed Israel's actions as defensive and proportionate, arguing that

---

[5] Candace Owens, X posts and YouTube commentary, September–November 2025.

Israel faces existential threats from Hamas, Hezbollah, and Iran. Following Israeli operations against Hezbollah leadership, he wrote, "Hezbollah's leadership is dead, its weapons caches largely destroyed, all at an insanely low military cost to Israel."[6] For Shapiro, such outcomes demonstrate not aggression, but restraint coupled with necessity.

Shapiro has also rejected moral equivalence between Israel and its adversaries, criticizing Western activists and campus protesters as "historically and morally illiterate Hamas sympathizers."[7] His defense is not primarily theological, but civilizational: Israel is portrayed as a liberal democracy defending itself against genocidal movements in a hostile region.

Ted Cruz

Running parallel to this political defense is a theological argument advanced by prominent evangelical leaders and politicians. Senator Ted Cruz has articulated this position explicitly,

---

[6] Ben Shapiro, X (formerly Twitter), November 27, 2024.

[7] Ben Shapiro, X thread addressing campus protests and Hamas, October 21, 2024.

grounding his unwavering support for Israel in the biblical promise of Genesis 12:3. In an interview, he stated that his Christian faith compels him to support Israel because "those who bless Israel will be blessed, and those who curse Israel will be cursed."[8] Cruz acknowledged uncertainty about the precise biblical reference, later associating it with Numbers 24:9, but nevertheless framed the principle as non-negotiable for U.S. foreign policy.[9]

This interpretation is widely shared. Figures such as John Hagee, Charlie Kirk, Mike Pence, Lindsey Graham, and Nikki Haley have all invoked the same promise to justify political and military support for the modern state of Israel.[10]

Pastor Hagee has repeatedly warned that nations opposing Israel invite divine judgment, while the late Kirk had posted Genesis 12:3 alongside imagery of the modern Israeli state, implying a

---

[8] Ted Cruz, interview with Tucker Carlson, June 2025.

[9] Ted Cruz, subsequent clarification on biblical reference, June 2025.

[10] Public statements and advocacy by John Hagee, Charlie Kirk, Mike Pence, Lindsey Graham, and Nikki Haley, 2023–2025.

direct continuity between Abrahamic blessing and contemporary geopolitics.[11]

Critics—including Carlson himself—have challenged this application, noting that the original promise was spoken to Abraham personally and questioning whether it can be transferred wholesale to a modern nation-state governed by secular leadership.[12] This theological dispute lies at the heart of the present controversy and exposes a deeper hermeneutical divide: whether biblical promises concerning Israel should be read spiritually, ethnically, eschatologically, or politically.

Beyond politics and theology, the debate has spilled into entertainment and popular culture. Celebrities such as Gal Gadot, Amy Schumer, Scarlett Johansson, and Ben Stiller have publicly affirmed Israel's right to exist and defend itself, often framing their support in terms of Jewish

---

[11] Charlie Kirk, X post invoking Genesis 12:3 with imagery of modern Israel, 2024.

[12] Tucker Carlson, interview questioning the application of Genesis 12:3 to the modern state of Israel, June 2025.

identity or opposition to antisemitism.[13] On the opposite side, figures such as Greta Thunberg and other activists have aligned themselves with pro-Palestinian movements that challenge Israel's legitimacy altogether.[14]

The voices surveyed above do not merely argue about Israel. They expose the unresolved question of what Israel is—and what, if anything, it proves.

A DIFFERENT APPROACH

Let me say clearly, what this book is **not** trying to do. It is not written to deny Israel's right to exist, nor to feed hostility toward Jews, nor to baptize any political platform. The question I am asking is narrower, more biblical, and—if we are honest—more demanding: **Do the biblical prophecies about Israel's "gathering" describe the same phenomenon as the modern return, or do they describe something else?**

---

[13] Public statements and social media posts by Gal Gadot, Amy Schumer, Scarlett Johansson, and Ben Stiller, 2023–2025.

[14] Public activism and protest participation by Greta Thunberg and affiliated pro-Palestinian movements, 2024–2025.

I have approached this subject with reverence: reverence for Scripture, and respect for the Jewish people. I also write as someone who has walked the land and taught there. It truly is amazing to see the archaeology and artifacts that attest to the veracity of the Bible. But visitors can't help but feel the gravity of age-old struggles that have taken place over thousands of years.

The stakes in discussing the modern State of Israel are not abstract. It is not merely an idea; Israel is a people, a place, a memory carried through centuries, and a flashpoint of modern fear and hope.

But do the prophets invite us to turn every crisis into a timetable? Jesus Himself warned against that posture—not because history is meaningless, but because the end of the age arrives through events that no one can schedule and no one can tame. The Bible never calls for people to obsess over charts, but to stay awake, stay faithful, and keep their lamps burning.

In other words, this book is not a rejection of prophecy. It is a plea to read prophecy carefully—without panic, without manipulation, and without confusing **what God has promised to do** with **what man is capable of building**.

10

As we research the formation of Modern Israel, we will see that human hands and minds were involved. But, should it be found that the modern state does not align with Bible prophecy, that would not in itself imply its formation was against God's will. And it would certainly not in itself indict the founders as being complicit in some kind of evil enterprise.

The voices and controversies surveyed above reveal the urgency of the present debate, but urgency alone cannot resolve it. Before judgments can be made— political, moral, or theological—the biblical framework itself must be examined. The question is not whether Israel matters, but how Scripture defines the meaning of Israel's restoration. It is to that framework that we now turn.

Introduction

The urgency of this discussion has intensified in recent years. Modern conflicts involving Israel have once again prompted a surge of prophetic speculation. Books, videos, and sermons have appeared claiming that we are witnessing the final sequence of history. Yet history offers sobering perspective: Previous generations were equally certain.

Wikipedia lists hundreds of predicted dates for apocalyptic events across various cultures and time periods in its article "List of dates predicted for apocalyptic events," often with numerous entries for each century demonstrating a vast history of such predictions. Within recent memory, Bible prophecy was invoked during world wars, during the Cold War, and during earlier Middle Eastern crises. The modern evangelical imagination has been shaped decisively by dispensational premillennialism. In this system, biblical prophecy is often treated as a roadmap of discrete events, many of which are believed to be observable within contemporary history.

13

Wars, treaties, and geopolitical tensions are read not merely as historical contingencies, but as indicators of prophetic acceleration. What is rarely acknowledged, however, is that this way of reading prophecy depends on a series of interpretive moves that are neither self-evident nor, historically, universal.

Much like political positions, these assumptions are rarely argued for. They are inherited.

THE PROPHETIC PROFILE IN SCRIPTURE

When one reads the prophetic texts themselves— Isaiah, Jeremiah, Ezekiel, Zechariah—the pattern is remarkably consistent. Israel's regathering is not described as an ambiguous or partial event. It is described as a moment when God acts openly, decisively, and universally.

The nations are affected. Creation responds. Wickedness is judged. The knowledge of the Lord spreads. The Davidic king reigns. The covenant is renewed. Death itself is addressed.

This is why Second Temple Jewish expectation, as reflected in apocalyptic literature and later rabbinic reflection, anticipated a redemption that would be unmistakable. However varied the details, the shape of the hope was clear: when God restores Israel, the world will know it. That conceptual shift matters profoundly for Christian interpretation.

When Christian theology absorbed the assumptions that undergirded the Jewish "Messianic Activism" Movement—especially within dispensational frameworks—it became easier to treat political milestones as prophetic fulfillments, even when the biblical descriptions far exceed what those milestones actually accomplish. The reestablishment of a Jewish homeland, the revival of Hebrew, and the survival of the state through conflict were increasingly spoken of as proof that prophetic regathering had begun.

But **proof** requires **criteria**.

Ironically, classical Jewish expectation and early Christian interpretation share a common restraint that modern prophecy enthusiasm often lacks. Both traditions expected redemption to be unmistakable. Both associated it with Messianic rule, judgment, and transformation. And both resisted identifying ordinary political events—however meaningful—as the fulfillment of ultimate hope.

WHAT SCRIPTURE ACTUALLY SAYS ABOUT "GATHERING"

When the prophets speak of Israel's gathering, they do so within a remarkably consistent framework. The gathering is not isolated from judgment; it follows it. It is not merely geographic; it is spiritual and moral. It is not accomplished quietly; it is accompanied by cosmic signs, the defeat of wicked powers, and the visible reign of God.

Isaiah does not describe a return to land while injustice persists unchecked and the nations continue unchanged. Ezekiel does not speak of bones coming together without breath, life, and covenant renewal. Jeremiah does not envision restoration apart from repentance and divine action. And Jesus, in His own teaching, places the gathering of the elect *after* tribulation, *after* cosmic disturbance, and *after* the appearing of the Son of Man.

Yet modern prophecy teaching often isolates the "return to the land" from the rest of that structure. What Scripture presents as a unified eschatological act is broken into stages, with the earliest stage identified with twentieth-century events and the remaining elements postponed indefinitely.

One reason Israel is so contested is that it sits at the intersection of **history** and **holy text**. And the moment Scripture is invoked, the debate changes. Israel becomes more than a nation; it becomes a sign—either of promises fulfilled or of prophecy misused. Yet remarkably few Christians can articulate *why* they believe what they believe about Israel.

That is exactly where confusion multiplies.

In later chapters we will observe dozens of Old Testament prophecies describing a "gathering" of Israel as a dramatic, God-driven event—tied to Messiah, judgment, and the restoration of all things

Contemporary Prophecy-talk and the "Headline Hermeneutic"

In the present moment, prophetic framing has surged again. Recent conflicts—especially the October 7, 2023 Hamas attack and the war that followed—have been interpreted by many voices through an apocalyptic lens, including bestselling popular works that explicitly connect contemporary events to Revelation's imagery and "end of days" narratives.

The most prominent example of this prophetic framing is Jonathan Cahn's recent books, including *The Dragon's Prophecy: Israel, the Dark Resurrection, and the End of Days* (2024). This work links contemporary events involving Israel (e.g., the October 7, 2023, attacks) to ancient prophecies, viewing the modern nation as central to apocalyptic unfoldings in Revelation and elsewhere.

Cahn posits that there is an unseen spiritual realm influencing global affairs, with a central focus on Israel as a key sign of the "End of Days." Key themes include, The "Dragon" (drawn from Revelation) as a symbolic dangerous force from ancient times now active in the world.

The "Dark Resurrection," referring to the revival of ancient entities or enmities paralleling Israel's modern resurrection as a nation.

The return of the "Sea Peoples" and other biblical motifs manifesting today. Hidden secrets of the apocalypse, including the "Colors of the Apocalypse," the "Day of the Dragon," and the role of "the Beast."

Cahn aims to reveal how these prophecies explain the mysteries of our chaotic times, what lies ahead, and practical spiritual keys for readers to gain victory over personal and global "dragons" (evils or conflicts). The book is presented as explosive and mind-blowing, intended to change how readers view the world and prepare for the future. The Dragon's Prophecy is preceded by over 50 years of novels that interpret the establishment of the modern State of Israel in 1948 as the fulfillment—or partial fulfillment—of biblical prophecies about the "regathering" of Israel in the last days (e.g., from passages in Deuteronomy 30, Isaiah 11, Ezekiel 36–37, and others).

Hal Lindsey's *The Late Great Planet Earth* (1970) is the seminal modern work in this genre, framing Israel's rebirth as a prophetic milestone tied to impending global events. Similar books that base discussions on this assumption: Hal Lindsey's own follow-ups and related works in the 1980s: *Countdown to Armageddon* (1980)—builds directly on *The Late Great Planet Earth*, linking Israel's modern existence to escalating end-times signs. *The Final Battle* (1995), *Apocalypse Code* (1997), and *Planet Earth 2000 A.D.* (1994)—continue interpreting current events, including Israel's role, as prophetic fulfillments.

Tim LaHaye and Jerry B. Jenkins' *Left Behind* series (1995–2007, starting with *Left Behind*) — Immensely popular fictional depictions of end-times prophecy, where the regathering of Israel and events in the Middle East play central roles in the rapture, tribulation, and Antichrist's rise. The *Left Behind* series and related nonfiction, like LaHaye's prophecy libraries, explicitly tie modern Israel to biblical promises.

David Reagan's *Israel in Bible Prophecy: Past, Present & Future* — Explores Israel's modern restoration as a key end-times sign, connecting it to prophecies of regathering and future blessing.

John Hagee's works, such as those associated with Christians United for Israel often frame Israel's 1948 establishment and ongoing conflicts as prophetic. Emphasizing Christian support for the nation as part of end-times fulfillment (e.g., in books like Jerusalem Countdown or related teachings).

These works generally share a futurist, literal interpretation of prophecy, distinguishing Israel from the Church and seeing the nation's modern regathering (often described as initially in "unbelief") as setting the stage for future events.

This perspective has fueled Christian Zionism and widespread evangelical interest in Middle East geopolitics as prophetic signs. These books all came on the heels of a religious trend of date setting that became vogue in the early 1900s.

Contemporary Date Setters

Below, I have listed individuals or groups who have predicted specific dates or narrow timeframes for the return of Christ (often tied to end-times events like the rapture, tribulation, or millennium)—since the era of early Zionism. They are submitted, somewhat for the purpose of injecting a little levity in the midst of an otherwise serious theological study. But the consequences were far from humorous to the thousands of people who were stumbled in their faith, or who made irreversible life decisions based on what turned out to be false information.

I've focused on predictions made from the time of late-19th-century Zionism onward. All have either failed, or for very recent ones, remain unfulfilled as of December 31, 2025.

Jehovah's Witnesses (founded by Charles Taze Russell): 1914 (initially for Armageddon and Christ's visible return; later reinterpreted as His invisible presence), with follow-up dates like 1918, 1925, 1975, and 1984 – Based on biblical chronology interpreting Daniel 4's "seven times" as 2,520 years from Jerusalem's fall in 607 BCE, marking the end of Gentile times and the start of God's kingdom; 1975 was tied to 6,000 years from Adam's creation; presumed to be in 4026 BCE.

John Chilembwe: 1915 – Predicted the millennium would begin amid colonial unrest in Africa, drawing from Revelation's prophecies of liberation and Christ's return to overthrow oppressors.

Sun Myung Moon (Unification Church): 1917–1930 (for Christ's advent, with Moon claiming to fulfill it himself!); also 1967 for the Kingdom of Heaven – Viewed himself as the "Lord of the Second Advent" called for by Jesus, based on divine revelations and prophecies of a new Messiah to complete Christ's mission; 1967 was linked to a major catastrophe and heavenly establishment.

Herbert W. Armstrong (Worldwide Church of God): 1936, 1943, 1972, and 1975 – Predicted great tribulation starting in these years, leading to Christ's return; calculations drew from British-Israelism (Anglo-Saxons as lost tribes of Israel), Daniel's prophecies, and a 19-year time cycle from 1934 when his ministry began; 1975 was seen as the end of 6,000 years of human rule.

Hal Lindsey: 1981 (initially for the rapture), 1988, and 2007 – Based on a biblical "generation" (40 years) from Israel's 1948 founding or 1967 Six-Day War recapture of Jerusalem (Matthew 24:32–34), plus alignments with astronomy, Soviet threats, and Revelation's prophecies; implied the rapture and tribulation would precede Christ's return within that timeframe.

Edgar C. Whisenant: September 11–13, 1988 (for the rapture), revised to 1989 and 1993 – Outlined "*88 reasons*" from biblical numerology, feast days (Rosh Hashanah), and calculations like 40 years from 1948, arguing the church age would end then, followed by tribulation and Christ's return seven years later.

Lee Jang Rim (Dami Missionary Church): October 28, 1992 – Predicted the rapture of 144,000 believers (from Revelation 7) at 9 a.m., based on numerology, visions, and end-times signs like earthquakes and wars; tied to supernatural evidence like camera anomalies.

Harold Camping (Family Radio): September 6, 1994; May 21, 2011 (for judgment/rapture); October 21, 2011 (for the end) – Used complex biblical math, like 7,000 years from Noah's flood (dated to 4990 BCE) or 5x10x17 symbolizing completeness; 2011 dates incorporated creation at 11,013 BCE and spiritual judgment starting in 1988.

Jerry Falwell: 1999–2009 – Stated Christ's return would likely occur within 10 years from 1999, based on Y2K fears, rising global chaos, and prophecies signaling the Antichrist's emergence (possibly a male Jew alive then).

Marilyn J. Agee: May 31, 1998 (Pentecost); September 12, 2007; April 6, 2008 – Drew from a 6,000-year cycle from Adam, plus 40 or 60 years from Israel's 1948 founding or 1967 war, aligned with Jewish feasts and astronomical signs like eclipses.

Ronald Weinland (Church of God): September 29, 2011; May 27, 2012; May 18, 2013; June 9, 2019 – Claimed to be one of Revelation's two witnesses; dates based on 1,260-day tribulation periods from 2008 economic events, tied to seals in Revelation and Christ's return on Pentecost.

Jack Van Impe: 2012 – Pointed to Mayan calendar alignments with biblical prophecies, global unrest, and end-times signs as indicating Christ's possible return.

Mark Biltz: September 28, 2015 – Linked Christ's return to a blood moon tetrad (lunar eclipses) on Jewish feasts, interpreting them as signs from Joel 2:31 and Revelation.

F. Kenton "Doc" Beshore: By 2021 – Argued for the rapture based on Psalm 90:10's 70–80-year generation from Israel's 1948 rebirth, with tribulation following.

Joshua Mhlakela: September 23–24, 2025; revised to October 7–8, 2025 – Claimed rapture dates via divine revelations, using Julian calendar adjustments and biblical feast alignments.

THE AUTHOR'S HEART FOR ISRAEL

I have been blessed to explore the Holy Land, to walk her streets and feel her pulse. I have Jewish friends, Jewish roots in my own ancestry, and a deep respect for the ethnos, which has historically preserved the testimony of the living God through millennia of suffering. I have personally seen most of Israel from the Finger of Galilee in the north to the Desert of Zin in the south. I have taught on location in Israel, including from the southern steps of the Temple Mount and from the top of the Megiddo Tell. As well as traveling the traditional route from Egypt, across the Red Sea, through Sinai.

The land of Israel truly is "Christian Disneyland" and I encourage all believers to visit Israel in order to affirm the veracity of Scriptures. Thus, this book is not born out of hostility, but of reverence—reverence for the Word of God, and for His faithfulness to every promise that He has spoken.

Yet, history teaches that zeal—religious or political—can confuse human innovation with divine actions. In the mid-nineteenth century, Rabbi Tsevi Hirsch Kalischer and others taught that divine redemption could be hastened by human effort, through settlement and cultivation of the Promised Land. Their "*proactive messianism*" laid the groundwork for modern religious Zionism and ultimately for the political birth of the State of Israel. Their hope was sincere; and their reasoning was rooted in Scripture to extent that a future gathering was certainly prophesied. But this human effort also signaled a major shift.

The Scriptures, however, tell a different story. The prophets and apostles spoke of a gathering not brought about by diplomacy, migration, or human strength, but by the direct intervention of the Messiah Himself—a gathering inseparable from resurrection, judgment, and the renewal of all things. This biblical restoration, the "ingathering of Israel," is not the work of man's hand, but the act of God at the end of the age.

The Proof about Israel explores this distinction carefully. It seeks to separate political Zionism from prophetic fulfillment, not to denounce the former but to clarify the latter. The book examines rabbinic sources, early Jewish writings, the New Testament witness, and the long-standing Christian understanding.

The biblical passages presented in the central section of this work form a cumulative testimony. From Isaiah to Zechariah, from Matthew to Revelation, they describe a day when the Lord Himself gathers His people, raises the dead, and judges the nations. This "proof" is not political—it is prophetic. It does not rest on headlines or treaties but upon the unchanging Word of God.

In a world increasingly divided by ideology and fear, it is crucial that the Church hold fast to both truth and compassion. This book therefore approaches the subject with humility and care. It affirms the dignity and destiny of Israel, yet reminds readers that the final restoration—the true gathering of God's people—awaits not the labor of men but the appearing of Christ, when every tribe and tongue will behold Him and the kingdoms of this world will become "the kingdom of our Lord and of His Christ."

This book speaks to that shared curiosity. It invites **believers, skeptics, and seekers alike** to examine Israel not merely as a nation among nations, but as a phenomenon that bridges the material and the spiritual, the ancient and the modern. Whether one approaches the subject through Scripture, through history, or through reason, the existence of Israel demands explanation. Why has this people endured, when even the greatest of empires have vanished? Why has this small land remained the focal point of world attention for three thousand years?

For **Christians**, Israel represents a thread running through the entire biblical narrative—from Abraham's covenant to Paul's vision of final restoration. For **Jews**, it embodies a living covenant still unfolding, a testimony to God's faithfulness amid centuries of exile. For **agnostics and atheists**, it is a case study in national survival against impossible odds—an intersection of history, identity, and collective purpose that transcends ordinary explanation.

This book does not assume agreement about divine intervention, but it does assume a shared human impulse to understand meaning. The claim that Israel's modern rebirth corresponds to biblical prophecy deserves examination, not dismissal. To believers, it may confirm the reliability of revelation. To skeptics, it may invite reflection on whether coincidence alone can account for so precise a pattern. The goal here is not to proselytize but to reason.

Beyond Apology or Advocacy

The Proof about Israel neither questions Israel's right to exist nor seeks to impose theological interpretations upon its politics.

It recognizes Israel's remarkable achievements: democratic resilience, scientific innovation, and the revival of Hebrew language and culture. But it also recognizes that admiration does not equate to prophetic fulfillment. The task is to distinguish between **Israel as a nation**—a legitimate political entity—and **Israel as a sign**, a motif woven through sacred Scripture.

The analysis therefore proceeds on two levels:

1. **Historical and sociopolitical** — tracing the evolution from early Zionist thought to the complexities of modern statehood.

2. **Theological and prophetic** — testing whether these developments align with the specific criteria of biblical restoration.

By separating these lenses, the reader is free to respect both without confusing them.

Ch. 1: From Vision to Movement

The nineteenth century stands as the hinge between prophetic hope and political realization. For nearly two millennia, the promise of Israel's restoration had been the province of prayer, poetry, and prophecy; now it began to take on the language of land grants, charters, and diplomatic correspondence. What the prophets described as the *day of the Lord* was gradually translated into a plan of colonization under the aegis of European powers.

This transformation did not occur in a vacuum. It was the product of several converging forces:

- **Religious restorationism** within Protestant Christianity, which viewed the return of the Jews as a sign of Christ's approaching kingdom.

- **Jewish religious nationalism,** which sought to end the long exile through self-initiative and the doctrine of "natural redemption."

- **European imperial expansion,** which made the Eastern Mediterranean a stage for strategic and spiritual ambition alike.

Each of these forces carried noble intentions. Yet together they created a movement that subtly replaced divine promise with the **Zionist enterprise.**

Before political Zionism had a name, it had a theology. Rabbi Tsevi Hirsch Kalischer, as noted earlier, taught that redemption could begin through practical steps: the purchase of land, agricultural settlement, and the revival of Hebrew life in Palestine. Kalischer's contemporary, Rabbi Yehuda Alkalai, spoke in similar tones from the Balkans, calling for a return to the land as a prelude to spiritual renewal. He wrote of a "process of awakening" that would culminate in divine deliverance—*if only Israel would first act in faith.*

Around the same time, **Moses Hess** (1812–1875), a secular philosopher and associate of Karl Marx, reframed these ideas for the modern age. In his 1862 book *Rome and Jerusalem,* Hess argued that Jewish emancipation in Europe would never suffice; national regeneration required the re-establishment of a homeland. His Zionism was not rooted in Scripture but in history and race. Yet the soil had been prepared by centuries of religious expectation. The line between covenant and nationalism was already blurred.

CHRISTIAN RESTORATIONISM AND BRITISH POLICY

While Jewish thinkers debated redemption's mode, British Protestants were busy giving it machinery. The **London Society for Promoting Christianity Amongst the Jews** (1809) had already planted a mission in Jerusalem by mid-century. Their dual aim—to evangelize Jews and to hasten prophecy—embodied the Restorationist conviction that the return to Zion would precede the Second Coming.

Men such as **Anthony Ashley-Cooper, the 7th Earl of Shaftesbury,** brought these hopes into the corridors of power. Shaftesbury's slogan, "A country without a nation for a nation without a country," captured the imperial mood of the age. His advocacy influenced Lord Palmerston and other British officials who viewed a Jewish return to Palestine as both a humanitarian gesture and a strategic foothold in the declining Ottoman Empire.

As will later be discovered within the *Colonial Times* memorandum of 1841, the language of prophecy was freely mixed with appeals to diplomacy. The "Protestant Powers of the North of Europe and America" were urged to participate in Israel's restoration as a sacred duty and a bulwark against Catholic and Islamic influence. Thus, theology became foreign policy; Restorationism became geopolitics.

EUROPEAN NATIONALISM AND THE JEWISH AWAKENING

Across the Continent, the spirit of nationalism was reshaping identities. Italians, Germans, and Hungarians sought unification; Poles and Greeks reclaimed sovereignty. Among Jews, long scattered and often marginalized, this same current stirred a new self-consciousness. The language of covenant blended with the rhetoric of nationhood.

The pogroms of the 1880s in Russia and Eastern Europe gave this awakening a tragic urgency. For many, return to Zion became not merely an act of faith but of survival. Yet even in its most pragmatic form, the dream retained religious undertones: the belief that settling the land of the fathers would summon divine favor.

THEODOR HERZL AND THE POLITICAL TURN

Into this ferment stepped **Theodor Herzl** (1860–1904), a Viennese journalist whose *Der Judenstaat* (1896) transformed the aspiration of centuries into a manifesto for statehood. Herzl's Zionism was overtly political, secular, and European in form. Yet he drew upon the emotional capital accumulated by religious Zionists and Christian restorationists alike.

When Herzl convened the **First Zionist Congress** in Basel (1897), he described his achievement in prophetic language:

> "At Basel I founded the Jewish State. Perhaps in five years, and certainly in fifty, everyone will recognize it."

His prediction proved eerily accurate. Fifty-one years later, in 1948, the State of Israel was declared. But what Herzl founded was not the messianic kingdom of Isaiah; it was a nation among nations, born of diplomacy and defended by arms. Its legitimacy as a state is undeniable. Yet its identification as the *fulfillment of prophecy* remains the question at the heart of this book.

By the early twentieth century, the convergence of imperial interest and biblical sentiment reached its apex in the **Balfour Declaration** of 1917. In a single paragraph addressed to Lord Rothschild, the British government expressed its support for "the establishment in Palestine of a national home for the Jewish people."

Prime Minister David Lloyd George, Foreign Secretary Arthur Balfour, and others involved in the decision were steeped in Restorationist thought. They saw themselves as instruments of divine destiny. Yet behind their idealism lay strategic motives: securing the Suez Canal, outmaneuvering the Ottomans, and ensuring British influence in the Middle East.

Thus, prophecy served politics, and politics in turn clothed itself in prophecy. The "times of restoration" once announced by Peter were now expressed through parliamentary language and military mandate.

By the mid-twentieth century, **religious Zionism** and **political Zionism** had joined hands. The former provided the moral vocabulary; the latter provided the machinery. When Israel declared independence in 1948, both camps claimed vindication. The rabbis saw divine providence; the statesmen saw historical necessity. The world saw a miracle.

Yet beneath the jubilation lay a theological tension unresolved since the nineteenth century: Was this return the *gathering of God's people at the end of the age*—or merely the latest chapter in Israel's long and unfinished history?

The modern State of Israel, though remarkable in survival and innovation, bears none of the marks of the Messianic Age described in Isaiah or Revelation. Its existence may signify divine patience, even preparation, but not yet the promised restoration of all things.

The blending of religious and political motives has left generations of believers uncertain how to interpret modern Israel. Some, following the dispensational charts, see the state's existence as incontrovertible proof of prophetic fulfillment. Others, recoiling from antisemitism and eager to affirm God's faithfulness, embrace Zionism uncritically. Still others, skeptical of both, view it as a purely secular enterprise.

The task of this study is not to assign blame but to restore perspective—to distinguish the **providential** from the **prophetic**, the **preparatory** from the **promised.** History may set the stage; but only Christ can open this end-times performance.

CONCLUSION: FROM PROMISE TO POLITICS

The story of Zionism's birth is thus the story of a profound inversion. The faith that once waited for heaven's descent learned to act on behalf of earth's ascent. Out of devotion came determination. Out of hope, came activism. Yet in the exchange, something essential and previously obvious was lost—the recognition that the kingdom of God cannot be legislated into being.

Israel's modern rebirth stands as a testimony to divine providence and human perseverance. But as this book will continue to show, **providence and**

prophecy are not identical. The one guides history through mercy; the other culminates it through glory. To confuse the two is to mistake the road for the destination.

Zionism in Context

Within Judaism itself, Zionism has never been monolithic. In the nineteenth century, traditional rabbis debated whether returning to the land before the Messiah was obedience or presumption. Some viewed settlement as sacred preparation, others, as an attempt to force God's hand. Since 1948, those debates have evolved. Many Jews now see the state as divine providence; others see it as a secular safeguard. This diversity of Jewish thought reveals a living faith wrestling with history—a struggle mirrored by Christians who, for two centuries, have read current events through prophetic eyes.

Understanding those parallel journeys—the **Jewish struggle, between "natural" and "miraculous" redemption**, and the **Christian struggle between Scripture and interpretation**—is essential to understanding the meaning of modern Israel.

The Christian attitude toward the Jewish people has also undergone dramatic change. From centuries of theological estrangement and Supersessionism, to nineteenth-century Restorationism, to twentieth-century Christian Zionism, the Church's view has shifted from antagonism to embrace—sometimes from guilt, sometimes from zeal, and often from both. Yet zeal, whether Jewish or Christian, can misinterpret the sequence.

The chapters that follow will trace that history— how prophecy, politics, and passion converged to shape our current understanding of Israel's role in the divine drama.

Israel beyond Prophecy

At the same time, this work recognizes that **Israel's legitimacy does not depend upon prophecy**.

A people's right to self-determination, safety, and cultural expression stands on universal moral grounds. Israel's moral and political acceptance must ultimately rest upon justice, human dignity, and the rule of law—principles that endure whether or not one believes in divine design.

A love for Israel need not require a timetable of Revelation; nor, does **honest critique of policy amount to disbelief in Scripture.**

The most durable acceptance of Israel will come when respect for her existence is rooted in conscience as well as covenant.

THE INQUIRY BEFORE US

Thus, the central inquiry of this book is threefold:

1. **For believers:** Does the modern State of Israel fulfill the prophetic promises of Scripture—or merely prefigure a greater gathering yet to come?

2. **For Jews:** How have traditional and modern forms of Zionism interpreted the tension between divine redemption and human initiative?

3. **For secular minds:** Does history itself point to a hidden hand behind the extraordinary survival and reconstitution of Israel, be it human or divine?

The Proof about Israel stands at the intersection of these questions. It neither defends nor denies; it seeks to discern. It invites every reader—religious or irreligious—to consider that perhaps Israel's story, whether viewed through faith or fact, continues to unfold.

The questions raised in these opening pages are not new. For more than two centuries, the world has wrestled with how to understand Israel's place among the nations—and, for many, how to reconcile that place with the words of Scripture. The very language used to frame the debate has evolved with time, mirroring the shifting tides of philosophy, politics, and faith.

In the eighteenth century, it was called *the Jewish Question*: a struggle to define the civic identity of a people long dispersed among Christian nations. In the age of empires, it became *the Palestine Question*: an inquiry into how two ancient peoples might share one contested land. And in our own era, it has matured—sometimes uneasily—into *the Israel Question*: a moral and spiritual reckoning with what the modern Jewish state represents to the world and to God.

Behind each of these phrases lies more than political theory. They reveal humanity's continuing effort to make sense of a story that refuses to end—a story that has outlasted monarchies, ideologies, and even the skepticism of modernity.

Each generation inherits the same riddle: how can a people once scattered to the ends of the earth not only endure, but also return? How can a promise spoken in the deserts of Sinai still shape the conscience of nations in the twenty-first century?

The following chapter traces that evolving conversation. It follows the "Israel Question" from its Enlightenment origins through the birth of Zionism and into the complex debates of our own time. By retracing this path, we begin to see how moral philosophy, political necessity, and theological conviction have converged—and often collided—in their attempts to explain the phenomenon of Israel.

Only by understanding that long journey can we approach the deeper inquiry of this book.

The rise of Zionism did not occur in isolation.

It emerged within a much longer conversation about Jewish identity, land, and legitimacy—one that predated modern nationalism and continues to shape global discourse today. To understand how Israel became a subject of perpetual moral inquiry, we must trace the evolution of the language used to describe it.

Ch. 2: The Evolution of the Israel Question

The phrase *"the Israel Question"* has come to represent one of the most enduring and complex discussions in modern history. It did not begin in our own century, nor even with the founding of the State of Israel. Its roots stretch back more than two hundred years to an Enlightenment-era Europe struggling to decide how an ancient, scattered people might fit within the new order of nation-states. Over time, what began as *the Jewish Question* evolved into *the Palestine Question*, and finally matured into what the modern world calls *the Israel Question.* Each transformation reflected the spirit of its age, yet all were bound by a single thread — the relationship between the Jewish people, their ancestral land, and the moral conscience of nations.

From the "Jewish Question" to National Aspiration

In eighteenth- and nineteenth-century Europe, the expression *the Jewish Question* referred to a pressing dilemma: how should Jews — long marginalized or confined to ghettos — be treated within societies built upon new ideals of citizenship, equality, and national identity? Philosophers and legislators debated whether Jews could become full citizens while retaining their religious distinctiveness.[15]

The phrase first appeared in British legal discussion surrounding the Jewish Naturalisation Act of 1753 and quickly spread across the Continent.[16] By the early nineteenth century, German thinkers such as Bruno Bauer asked whether emancipation was even possible without the abandonment of faith.[17] In this "question," theology and politics intertwined: could a people historically defined by covenant belong in a polity defined by creedless citizenship?

The issue deepened as the century progressed. The *Judenfrage* soon expanded from a civic concern into a national one. Was Judaism merely a religion? Or were the Jews a nation without a homeland? The rise of European nationalism — with its calls for

---

[15] Bruno Bauer, *Die Judenfrage* (Braunschweig: F. Vieweg, 1843).

[16] "The Jewish Naturalisation Act Debate," *The London Gazette*, 1753.

[17] Moses Hess, *Rome and Jerusalem: The Last National Question* (Leipzig: Eduard Mendelssohn, 1862).

linguistic and territorial unity — made this question unavoidable. To some, inclusion required assimilation; to others, difference was irreducible. As antisemitism hardened in Russia, Austria, and Germany, the "Jewish Question" began to acquire a darker connotation: that Jews themselves constituted a *problem* to be solved through conversion, expulsion, or worse. Thus, the "Jewish Problem" became an acceptable nomenclature.[18]

Within this climate, new answers arose. Writers and activists from Moses Hess to Theodor Herzl concluded that equality inside Christian Europe might never be secure. If modern nationalism required land, perhaps the Jews must reclaim their own.[19] The *Jewish Question* thus birthed the earliest visions of Zionism — a political and cultural project seeking not mere tolerance but restoration. What had been an issue of citizenship became an issue of nationhood.

The rhetorical habit of calling such matters a "question" carried moral weight. It implied that a

---

[18] Theodor Herzl, *Der Judenstaat* (Vienna: M. Brettauer, 1896).

[19] "Why Is the Jewish Question Different from All Similar Questions?" *Contending Modernities*, University of Notre Dame, accessed 2025.

people's very existence awaited the verdict of others. Later generations would inherit this linguistic frame, transferring it from the *Jewish Question* of emancipation to the *Palestine Question* of territorial governance, and finally to the *Israel Question* of state legitimacy.[20]

THE SHIFT TO THE "PALESTINE QUESTION"

By the late nineteenth century, as Jewish immigration increased under Ottoman rule, attention moved from European civil status to the destiny of a specific land. The *Palestine Question* arose from overlapping claims — religious, historical, and political — between Jews seeking return and Arabs asserting native identity. When the British Empire assumed control of the region after World War I, the phrase appeared frequently in diplomatic correspondence and League of Nations documents to describe the "problem" of governing a territory sacred to three faiths.[21]

---

[20] *League of Nations Mandate for Palestine*, 1922.

[21] United Nations, "Question of Palestine,"

Initially the issue carried a colonial tone: how should imperial powers manage immigration, property, and representation in a land promised by Scripture yet administered by mandate?

The Balfour Declaration of 1917, pledging support for a "national home for the Jewish people," intensified debate over whose rights would prevail. Arab nationalists, inspired by the same currents of self-determination sweeping post-war Europe, rejected what they viewed as European encroachment. Zionist leaders, meanwhile, argued that the declaration merely acknowledged a pre-existing historical claim.

During the inter-war years, the *Palestine Question* became the focal point of international diplomacy. It was discussed in White Papers, commissions, and finally in United Nations proceedings that considered partition.[22] By 1948, when Israel

---

UNISPAL Document A/RES/181(II), 1947. https://www.un.org/unispal/document/auto-insert-206581/

[22] Daniel Chernilo, "The Rise and Rise of the 'Israel Question,'" in *The New Jewish Question: Global Modernity and the State of Israel* (New York: Routledge/Taylor & Francis, 2024).

declared independence, the old civic debate — how Jews might live *within* other nations — had been replaced by a territorial one: how a Jewish nation might live *among* other nations.

This shift from minority status to national sovereignty marked a turning point in modern political thought. The moral categories that once applied to individuals now applied to states. Sympathy for a persecuted people gave way to scrutiny of a power capable of both defending and displacing populations. Thus, when Israel emerged, the world inherited a new formulation — *the Israel Question*.

THE BIRTH OF "THE ISRAEL QUESTION"

After 1948 the conversation changed once again. What had been the "Jewish Question" of emancipation and the "Palestine Question" of administration became, in the post-war world, the *Israel Question* — a debate about the character and legitimacy of the state itself.

No longer concerned primarily with whether Jews deserved a homeland, observers now asked how that homeland conducted itself: Could a state be both

Jewish and *democratic*? How should it treat its Arab citizens and Palestinian neighbors? Where were its borders to be drawn, and upon what moral or legal foundations did its authority rest?

By the late twentieth century scholars such as Daniel Chernilo argued that the *Israel Question* represented "a twenty-first-century incarnation of earlier Jewish questions," recast from the level of individual rights to that of state identity.[23]

In this new form, the "question" encompassed not only Israel's internal politics but also its standing within international law and global norms. Critics spoke of occupation and human rights, defenders of security, and self-determination.

Both, however, inherited the same conceptual grammar: Israel was again treated as a subject to be judged by the tribunal of world opinion.

---

[23] "Israel and the Jewish Question," *MERIP Reports*, no. 131 (March 1985). https://merip.org/1985/03/israel-and-the-jewish-question/.

The persistence of anti-Semitic tropes complicated this discourse. Even sincere critiques of policy sometimes revived the same rhetoric of suspicion, once aimed at Jews in exile. As one scholar observed: "Whether as a national Jewish question or an international Israel question, similar patterns of hostility are mobilized under new vocabularies."[24]

---

[24] "The Israel Question after Trump—and Before," *Studies in American Jewish Literature* 39, no. 1 (2020): 93–107. https://www.jstor.org/stable/10.5325/studamerjewilite.3 9.1.0093.

From the Jewish Question to the Israel Question

Approximate date	Phrase / Usage	Main referent	Key shift
1750s - early 1800s	"Jewish Question"	Jews in Europe (civil/legal status)	Minority integration/emancipation
mid-19th C	"Judenfrage" in Germany/Austria	Jews as a "nation" or not, assimilation vs difference	National question dimension introduced
Late 19th – early 20th C	"Palestine Question"	Territory (Palestine), Jewish immigration/Zionism, Arab nationalism	From minority to territory/nation
Post-1948 (state of Israel) onward	"Israel Question" begins to appear (increasing by late 20th & 21st C)	State of Israel: its identity, legitimacy, relations, global role	From territory to state/legitimacy/international norms
21st C	"Israel Question" as global norm/human-rights frame	Israel in world politics; Zionism; anti-Zionism/antisemitism debate	From state to global normative contestation

The Modern Question: A Global Debate

In the twenty-first century, *the Israel Question* has expanded far beyond the borders of the Middle East. It is now argued in parliaments, universities, churches, and on social media platforms—each arena reflecting the tensions of a world still struggling to balance history, justice, and faith. The term has become a cipher for multiple conversations at once: the legitimacy of Israel's statehood, the rights of Palestinians, the boundaries of criticism and antisemitism, and the moral standing of nations that helped create the present order.

At times, the phrase functions as a mask for ancient prejudices—antipathy toward Jews repackaged in secular form. At other times, it is a genuine inquiry into reconciliation and coexistence. The modern "question" thus operates on several levels: moral, diplomatic, and theological. It asks not merely whether Israel has the right to exist, but on what basis nations themselves claim moral legitimacy in a post-colonial, globalized age.

As historian Daniel Chernilo notes, the *Israel Question* has moved from questions of *territory* to questions of *norms*: from disputes about land to debates about the principles by which the international community measures justice. Within this frame, Israel's policies are weighed in human-rights courts, and its identity debated in academic symposia that often echo the ideological clashes once heard in the salons of nineteenth-century Europe. The continuity is striking: each generation returns to the same inquiry—how the existence of Israel tests the moral boundaries of modernity itself.

The persistence of this framing reveals something deeper than politics. Few modern nations have had their very existence phrased as a "question." In that sense, Israel is exceptional not only in origin, but also in perception. The world continues to ask what Israel *means*, not merely what it *does*. This ongoing scrutiny exposes a moral discomfort with election, distinctiveness, and the intertwining of faith and history—concepts that challenge the secular assumptions of modern thought.

CONTINUITY AND SIGNIFICANCE

The endurance of this "Question" across three centuries—Jewish, Palestinian, and Israeli—suggests that it is *more* than a matter of policy or diplomacy. It reflects an underlying tension between transcendence and politics, between a people defined by covenant and a world governed by reason of state.

From the *Jewish Question* emerged the struggle for belonging; from the *Palestine Question,* the contest for land; and from the *Israel Question,* the search for legitimacy. Each stage carries the residue of the last. What began as a moral question about integration has become a geopolitical question about existence itself.

To study this progression is to glimpse how the world measures its own conscience. The treatment of Israel—once of Jews as citizens, later of Jews as a nation, now of Israel as a state—serves as a mirror reflecting humanity's engagement with justice, faith, and destiny.

The language of "question" betrays not only uncertainty about Israel but about the world's own moral bearings.

Thus, the *Israel Question* is not solely about the Jewish people or their land; it concerns the nations that stand as witnesses to their story. It reveals how modern civilization wrestles with the meaning of promise and purpose in history. The debate over Israel, for all its political immediacy, remains a continuation of a far older dialogue—one that began when humanity first confronted the idea: that history itself might serve a moral design.

It is at this intersection of history and meaning that *The Proof about Israel* takes its stand. The modern *Israel Question,* though wrapped in political debate and international controversy, cannot be fully understood apart from the larger moral narrative of which it forms a part. Behind each linguistic shift— from the *Jewish Question* to the *Palestine Question* to the *Israel Question*—lies a continuity of purpose: the unfolding of human history toward moral accountability.

This book therefore turns from the rhetoric of nations to the deeper question of identity and purpose. What defines a people's calling? What marks the difference between restoration and mere survival? The inquiry is not confined to theology; it is an examination of how moral expectation and political reality converge in our own age. The historical path traced in this chapter leads naturally to the nineteenth-century Restorationist movement—the moment when Christian thinkers began to interpret the Jewish return to their ancestral land as evidence of prophetic fulfillment.

Chapter 3 explores that awakening in both Jewish and Christian circles: how hope, scholarship, and eschatology intertwined to shape the modern imagination of Israel's rebirth. Only by understanding that intellectual and spiritual preparation can we discern how today's *Israel Question* continues to echo the expectations first kindled in that era.

Ch. 3: The Restorationist Awakening

The centuries following the Reformation witnessed a remarkable shift in Christian thinking about the Jewish people and the fulfillment of prophecy.

Early Protestant theologians, returning to Scripture rather than tradition, rediscovered the apostolic language of *restoration* and *refreshing* in Peter's sermon recorded in Acts 3:19–21:

> "Repent therefore and be converted, that your sins may be blotted out, so that times of refreshing may come from the presence of the Lord, and that He may send Jesus Christ, who was preached to you before, whom heaven must receive until the times of restoration of all things, which God has spoken by the mouth of all His holy prophets since the world began."

From this passage arose what became known as the **Restoration Movement**—a Protestant missionary conviction that the Second Coming of Christ might be hastened by the conversion of the Jews.

If repentance and restoration were the conditions for Christ's return, then surely, they reasoned, the conversion and return of Israel must be the prelude to the "times of refreshing" spoken of by St. Peter. The logic was simple and, to its proponents, irresistible: Jesus would remain at the right hand of the Father *until* the "restoration of all things." Therefore, if the Church could help restore the Jews to faith in their Messiah, the final sequence of prophetic events might begin.

The **Restorationists** thus drew a direct connection between the salvation of Israel and the consummation of the age. Their prayers and labors were not political, but evangelistic—motivated by compassion for a people long despised and by an eschatological hope that "all Israel shall be saved." They envisioned Jewish repentance not as an isolated revival but as the spark of a cosmic renewal, the harbinger of Christ's return.

Before this time, the wider Church had generally regarded the Jews as a people left in spiritual blindness, tragically separated from grace by unbelief. But the Restorationist era saw a change in tone and purpose. The question was no longer, *whether* Jews might believe, but *how the nations might help them do so.* By the early nineteenth century, the emphasis began to shift again—from individual conversion to the notion of **national restoration**—that the Jewish people might not only believe but also return physically to the land of their fathers.

The Christian Roots of Early Zionism

Contrary to many modern assumptions, the earliest momentum toward a Jewish return to Palestine came not from Jewish financiers or secret councils, but from Christian evangelicals in England and Scotland who read the Bible literally and longed for its fulfillment.

In 1809, British evangelicals founded *The London Society for Promoting Christianity Amongst the Jews*. Their aim was not merely proselytism but participation in prophecy. They established missions, printed Hebrew New Testaments, and even organized a permanent presence in Jerusalem—anticipating the modern missionary model that would later characterize nineteenth-century Christianity.

Meanwhile, Scottish Presbyterians, stirred by similar convictions, organized a *Mission of Inquiry to the Jews* in Palestine. The expedition, led by the Reverends Robert Murray McCheyne and Andrew Bonar, was both investigative and pastoral. Their findings, published as *Narrative of a Visit to the Holy Land and Mission of Inquiry to the Jews* (1843), described a Jewish remnant living in great poverty under Ottoman and later Egyptian rule. The travelers reported meeting elderly Jews who had journeyed to Jerusalem in their final years simply to die and be buried in sacred soil—testimony to an undying hope for return, even before the rise of political Zionism.

McCheyne and Bonar's narrative stirred English hearts. Within a few years, the idea of restoring the Jews to their ancient homeland became a matter of public conversation and parliamentary notice. This early *Christian Zionism*—long before Theodor Herzl or the Basel Congress—was animated by prophecy rather than politics.

THE MEMORANDUM TO THE PROTESTANT POWERS (1841)

By the 1830s, British Restorationism had matured into a theological and diplomatic movement. The most striking evidence of this appeared in the form of a formal document published on the front page of the *Colonial Times* on February 23, 1841, under the title *Memorandum to the Protestant Powers of the North of Europe and America.*

The memorandum—addressed to Queen Victoria, the Kings of Prussia, Denmark, Sweden, Hanover, and others—urged the Protestant nations to recognize the providential importance of the Jewish people and to assist in their physical and spiritual restoration. It opened with a solemn invocation:

> "The Most High God, who reigns in the kingdoms of men … having in these days granted a season of repose to His witnessing church … the days are drawing near when the dominion, and the glory, and the kingdom … shall serve Him who cometh in the clouds of heaven."

Throughout, its authors appealed to Scripture as both authority and prophecy fulfilled in their own generation. They cited Daniel, Isaiah, Revelation, and Deuteronomy, proclaiming:

"The fig-tree putteth forth her leaves again... Israel's sons are asking the way to Zion, by which we know that the summer is at hand."

The memorandum declared that the "days draw nigh" when "under the hallowed sway of Messiah the Prince, the now despised nation of the Jews shall possess the kingdom." It called upon Protestant monarchs to act as instruments of divine providence:

"He that scattered Israel will gather him, and keep him as a shepherd doth his flock (Jeremiah 31:10)... Who is there among you, high and mighty ones of all the nations, to fulfill the good pleasure of the Lord of Heaven, saying to Jerusalem, 'Thou shalt be built,' and to the temple, 'Thy foundations shall be laid'?"

Even in its political appeals, the memorandum was overtly theological. It spoke not of conquest or colonization but of offering the Jewish people "as an offering to the Lord of Hosts in Mount Zion."

Signatories sent copies of the document to heads of state across Europe and America. The British Foreign Secretary, Lord Palmerston, formally presented it to Queen Victoria, noting in his March 14, 1839 reply:

"Her Majesty has been graciously pleased to receive the same."

The memorandum's influence cannot be overstated. It framed the restoration of the Jews as both a Christian duty and a prophetic necessity, blending millenarian expectation with British evangelical activism. This was not political Zionism as it would later develop under Herzl, but a **religious pre-Zionism**—an eschatological movement believing that God would use Protestant nations as the "Cyrus" of a new age.

PUBLIC SYMPATHY AND THE MORAL CAUSE

The Restorationist vision soon found a sympathetic echo in the British press. An open letter to *The Times* of London captured both the moral and prophetic dimensions of this new awakening:

"Every right-minded person must feel gratified at the general expression of interest in the Jewish nation… It would be a noble thing for a Christian nation to restore these wanderers to their homes again. It would be a crowning point in the glory of England to bring about such an event."

The letter reminded readers that the Jews' homelessness was not merely a geopolitical tragedy but a theological challenge:

"The wild bird hath her nest, the fox his cave,
Mankind their country—Israel but the grave."

To aid the Jews' return, the writer argued, would be to participate in divine justice: "The special blessings promised in the Scriptures to those who befriend the Jews would rest upon her [England]."

This popular appeal, sentimental and prophetic in equal measure, reveals how deeply biblical literalism had intertwined with Victorian philanthropy. By the mid-nineteenth century, the expectation that Protestant powers might help replant Israel in her land had become a mainstream notion among revivalist churches and mission societies.

From Restorationism to Religious Zionism

Thus, by the time Rabbi Tsevi Hirsch Kalischer began advocating "natural redemption" through Jewish colonization of Palestine, the soil of Europe—both Christian and Jewish—was already primed for the idea. Kalischer's proposals, though Jewish in origin, echoed a century of Protestant longing that had already looked toward Zion as the stage of God's final acts.

In his book *Derishat Zion* (Seeking Zion, 1862), Kalischer wrote:

> "Is it fitting for us to remain passive and say, 'Let the Holy One, blessed be He, accomplish it,' while we ourselves do nothing? No, we must begin the redemption ourselves; for only when we take the first step will God complete it."

This concept of *"beginning the redemption"* became the cornerstone of modern religious Zionism. It recast messianic expectation as a **national project**, shifting the focus from repentance to settlement, from covenant renewal to land reclamation.

For the first time since antiquity, the return to Zion was conceived not as a divine rescue but as a human initiative to which divine approval would be added. It was, in essence, a theology of **redemption by development.**

Christian Restorationism and Jewish Religious Zionism were, in this sense, parallel rivers flowing from a common spring: the conviction that prophecy was about to be fulfilled. The crucial difference lay in the means—whether the restoration would come by divine intervention or by human initiative.

The next chapters of *The Proof about Israel* will examine how that question—divine versus human agency—became the fault line between prophetic faith and political theology. From the pulpit of C. H. Spurgeon to the theories of John Nelson Darby, and through the fervor of nineteenth-century Dispensationalism, we will trace how the hope for Israel's salvation evolved into competing visions of God's timetable—and how those visions continue to shape our interpretation of Israel's role in prophecy today.

Ch. 4: The Shift from Salvation to Nationalism

By the mid-nineteenth century, the Restorationist movement had achieved what earlier centuries could scarcely have imagined: a widespread sympathy for the Jewish people and a serious reconsideration of their prophetic role. Yet as theological interest turned into political activism, the meaning of *restoration* itself began to change. What had once meant repentance and renewal of faith gradually came to mean re-establishment of sovereignty and statehood.

This transformation—subtle at first—would eventually redirect both Christian theology and Jewish nationalism.

SPURGEON'S CAUTIOUS HOPE

Among evangelical voices of the age, none carried greater weight than **Charles Haddon Spurgeon**, the "Prince of Preachers." Spurgeon believed passionately that God still had purposes for Israel, but he did not equate the nation's political re-emergence with prophetic fulfillment. For him,

Israel's future hope rested not in human settlement but in spiritual awakening.

From his pulpit at the Metropolitan Tabernacle, Spurgeon preached:

> "There will be a native government again; there will again be the form of a body politic; a state shall be incorporated; and a king shall reign. Israel has now become alienated from her own land. But her sons shall again return to their own borders. Yet, let us never forget, the **main point of the promise is spiritual.** Their hearts must be changed before their condition can be changed."

Spurgeon's balance of literal and spiritual expectation reflected the lingering humility of the older Restorationists. He hoped for Israel's return, but only under the lordship of her Messiah. He saw in the Jewish people a testimony to divine faithfulness, not a mandate for premature sovereignty. To Spurgeon, the promise of restoration was not an argument for nationalism but a prophecy of redemption—a work that only Christ Himself could accomplish.

Meanwhile, another current was gaining strength, carried forward by **John Nelson Darby**, a former Anglican clergyman and a founder of the Plymouth Brethren movement. Darby's system of *Dispensationalism* reorganized biblical prophecy into a series of distinct epochs, each governed by a different divine administration. Within this scheme, Israel and the Church were no longer two stages of one redemptive plan, but two separate peoples with divergent destinies.

In Darby's framework, the Church was a temporary "parenthesis" in God's dealings with Israel. The promises of land, kingdom, and blessing would be fulfilled literally to the Jewish nation *after* the Church had been removed from the earth through a secret "rapture." This new interpretive model appealed to a generation eager for clarity amid the confusion of modernity, but it also fractured the unity of biblical redemption.

Darby's writings reached America through the prophetic conferences of the 1870s and 1880s, eventually influencing such figures as D. L. Moody, C. I. Scofield, and countless evangelical pastors. The

Scofield Reference Bible (1909) would codify Darby's system, ensuring its dominance in twentieth-century evangelical thought.

Yet, for all its ingenuity, Darby's theology subtly reversed the order of apostolic expectation. Whereas Peter had spoken of a single restoration accomplished by the return of Christ, Dispensationalism envisioned a partial restoration *before* His coming—a geopolitical revival that would pave the way for tribulation and final judgment. In this model, human history, rather than divine intervention, became the stage upon which prophecy was progressively fulfilled.

FROM THEOLOGICAL EXPECTATION TO POLITICAL AGENDA

As these new prophetic frameworks spread, the line between spiritual hope and political action grew increasingly blurred. The expectation of Israel's restoration became less a prayer for repentance and more a chart of future events. In some circles, the gathering of the Jews to Palestine was no longer the outcome of faith but a *precondition* for the Second Coming. Traditional Christian denominations rejected Darby's unconventional parsing of

Scriptures. Perhaps Dispensationalism's most glaring "tragic flaw" was placing Jacob's Trouble *after* the Fullness of the Gentiles contrary to Luke 21:24, which shows Jacob's Trouble persisting up "*until* the times of the Gentiles are fulfilled."

Nevertheless, by the late nineteenth century, Dispensationalism's theological momentum converged with Jewish nationalism. The same Scriptures that inspired Restorationist prayer meetings now fueled diplomatic proposals and colonization plans. When Theodor Herzl convened the First Zionist Congress in 1897, he did so in a world already primed by decades of Christian prophecy conferences, missionary reports, and popular sermons proclaiming, "The fig tree putteth forth her leaves."

The transformation was complete: what had begun as a call to evangelize and comfort Israel had become a program to re-establish her politically. The Restorationist plea for Jewish conversion had matured into a geopolitical project—one that would eventually bear fruit in the creation of the modern State of Israel in 1948.

Two Visions of Restoration

It is important to understand that these developments did not arise from hostility to Scripture, but from differing ways of interpreting its timing and agency.

- The **Restorationists** believed that spiritual revival among the Jews would bring the Messiah.
- The **Dispensationalists** believed that the re-gathering of the Jews would precede His return.
- Both claimed fidelity to the prophets; both desired the glory of God. Yet one placed its hope in divine initiative, the other in a human movement.

Between these poles lies the central question of this book: **Is the modern return of Israel the fulfillment of prophecy—or merely the prelude to a fulfillment yet to come?**

Closing the Nineteenth-Century Circle

By the end of the Victorian era, Christian theology had sown the seeds of modern Zionism. Sermons, missionary journals, and prophetic tracts spoke with confidence of Israel's "restoration."

Few paused to ask whether the restoration of land without the Lord could satisfy the Scriptures that foretold it. The Messianic hope—once centered upon the visible, glorious return of Christ—was now entangled with the ambitions of men.

As this book proceeds, we will return to that question repeatedly: how the language of prophecy was re-interpreted, how national aspiration replaced spiritual anticipation, and how the biblical promise of a divine gathering became the political narrative of a modern state. For now, it is enough to observe that the nineteenth century closed with two competing visions of redemption:

1. one **from heaven downward**, awaiting the return of Christ to restore all things;
2. the other **from earth upward**, striving through human endeavor to prepare His way.

History would soon reveal which vision bore the proof of divine authorship.

Ch. 5: The Messianic Age and Its Misconceptions

"They shall not hurt nor destroy in all My holy mountain, for the earth shall be full of the knowledge of the Lord as the waters cover the sea."
— Isaiah 11: 9

TWO ROADS TOWARD THE SAME HORIZON

Few doctrines have been more eagerly anticipated, and more widely misunderstood, than the Messianic Age. Across both Jewish and Christian traditions, it stands as the radiant horizon of history: the era when injustice is decisively judged, the nations are reordered under divine authority, and the knowledge of God fills the earth without rival. Yet precisely because of its importance, the Messianic hope has often been compressed, reinterpreted, or prematurely applied to ordinary political events.

The prophets do not describe the Messianic Age as a modest improvement of conditions or as the gradual moral ascent of civilization. They describe a rupture—an interruption of history by the direct action of God. The Messiah does not merely preside over reform; He *establishes* righteousness. Violence does not merely decline; it ceases. Knowledge of the LORD does not expand through education alone; it floods the world with the inevitability of a tide.

Despite this clarity, history records repeated attempts to approach that bright-light horizon by two different roads. One road waits for God to act decisively from heaven. The other seeks to prepare the ground through human initiative. Both claim fidelity to Scripture. Both speak the language of hope. Yet they diverge sharply in how they understand agency, timing, and proof.

CLASSICAL JEWISH EXPECTATION

Classical Redemption by Divine Intervention

For most of Jewish history, the Messianic Age was not expected to arise through ordinary political success. Classical rabbinic literature, while diverse in detail, is unified in one essential conviction:

redemption would be unmistakably *divine*. The Messiah would not emerge as the natural culmination of human effort, but as the intervention of God into history.

This expectation is reflected in the Talmudic warnings against "forcing the end" (*ketz*). The concern was not that human action was evil in itself, but that mistaking human initiative for divine fulfillment could distort faith and invite disaster. The Messiah would come when God acted—not when circumstances appeared favorable.

Biblical prophecy reinforced this restraint. Isaiah portrays the Messianic reign as inseparable from judgment, the overthrow of wickedness, and the visible establishment of righteousness. Ezekiel's vision of restoration culminates not in settlement, but in resurrection—dry bones receiving breath by the Spirit of God. Zechariah links Jerusalem's renewal to the LORD Himself standing on the Mount of Olives, splitting the ground and reigning as King over all the earth. In these texts, restoration is not ambiguous. It does not arrive quietly. It is not mistaken for ordinary history. When redemption comes, all creation responds.

The Emergence of "Natural Redemption" in Jewish Thought

This traditional posture began to shift in the nineteenth century. Under the pressures of European nationalism, emancipation, and persecution, new theological categories emerged within Judaism. Chief among them was the concept of *natural redemption*—the belief that God might advance His redemptive purposes through secular historical processes before their spiritual culmination.

Rabbi Abraham Isaac Kook articulated this view most influentially. In his thought, secular Zionism—though outwardly irreligious—could function as an unconscious instrument of divine will. Agricultural labor, political organization, and territorial settlement were no longer merely preparatory acts; they were recast as the early stages of redemption itself.

> "Our constant goal is not only to be redeemed from Egypt, not only to be healed from wounds and delivered from disease, not only to come forth from the bonds of poverty and the darkness of blindness. We yearn to be filled with greatness: with the great wealth of the soul. We thirst for a fresh life, filled with

brilliance. And we come to the land of Israel. We hope for redemption, we pine for a redemption of the soul, so that the unveiling will be total, so that rays of eternal life will stream from the source of the holy of holies, from the source of the love of pleasure of the eternal Rock, who illumines the lovely land for us with beams of glory."[25]

This reflects Rav Kook's philosophy of natural redemption (*geulah ha-tiv'it*), where the return to and revival in Eretz Yisrael is part of an organic, gradual process that unites the physical ingathering of exiles with the highest spiritual elevation, drawing divine light into the world through the land itself.

This was a significant theological innovation. Redemption, once expected as a sudden act of God, was now permitted to unfold gradually through human effort. The Messiah's arrival remained future, but the process leading to it was already underway.

---

[25] Rabbi Abraham Isaac Kook, *Moadei Harayah*.

NINETEENTH-CENTURY MESSIANIC ACTIVISM

During the middle decades of the nineteenth century, a small but influential circle of European rabbis began to articulate a new understanding of Jewish redemption. Among the most prominent figures in this development was **Tsevi Hirsch Kalischer**, a Polish-German rabbi whose writings helped lay the intellectual groundwork for what would later be known as religious Zionism.

Early Correspondence and Theological Foundations

Kalischer's shift toward activism can be traced to the late 1830s, when he composed a lengthy letter addressed to Lionel de Rothschild, urging him to support Jewish resettlement in Palestine. Written entirely in Hebrew and Aramaic, the letter was not a personal appeal in the modern sense, but rather a carefully constructed theological treatise. Drawing on biblical exegesis, halakhic argumentation, and historical reflection, Kalischer presented redemption as a process unfolding through identifiable human agents rather than sudden supernatural intervention.[26]

---

[26] Tsevi Hirsch Kalischer, *Derishat Tsiyon* (1862).

Central to his argument was the conviction that divine providence operates through prominent individuals positioned to influence history. In this respect, Rothschild was not merely a benefactor but a potential instrument of God's purposes. The tone and structure of the letter closely resemble rabbinic scholarship rather than private correspondence, underscoring Kalischer's intent that its reasoning be evaluated on theological rather than emotional grounds.

Derishat Tsiyon and the Turn to Public Advocacy

Kalischer's ideas reached a broader audience with the publication of *Derishat Tsiyon* ("Seeking Zion") in 1862. Issued by the Kolonisations-Verein für Palästina (Society for the Settlement of Palestine), the work expanded upon his earlier correspondence and presented a sustained argument for Jewish agricultural settlement in the Land of Israel. Its publication marked Kalischer's transition from local rabbinic leadership to international advocacy.

In *Derishat Tsiyon*, Kalischer argued that redemption should not be imagined as an abrupt miracle. Rather, he insisted that the prophetic promises would be fulfilled gradually through human initiative, economic preparation, and settlement of the land. The restoration of Jewish life in Palestine was therefore not a sign of premature presumption but a necessary preliminary stage in the redemptive process. This perspective represented a significant departure from dominant rabbinic caution regarding human attempts to hasten redemption.[27]

The book attracted both supporters and critics, prompting Kalischer to engage extensively with the expanding Jewish press of Europe. He wrote articles, published responses to objections, solicited rabbinic endorsements, and maintained correspondence with readers across the continent.[28] Subsequent editions of *Derishat Tsiyon*, including a German translation and a revised Hebrew version published in 1866, incorporated additional material reflecting these debates and practical developments.

---

[27] Philip Earl Steele, "Rabbi Kalischer from Toruń – the Father of Religious Zionism," Jewish Heritage Europe, December 20, 2021.

[28] Kalischer, Derishat Tsiyon, quoted in Steele, "Rabbi Kalischer from Toruń," describing redemption as arriving "by slow degrees."

Organizational Efforts and Practical Challenges

The publication of *Derishat Tsiyon* coincided with Kalischer's direct involvement in organizational initiatives aimed at translating theory into practice. During the late 1850s and early 1860s, he played a leading role in the Kolonisations-Verein für Palästina, headquartered in Frankfurt, which sought to promote Jewish agricultural settlement in Ottoman Palestine.

Following the dissolution of the society in 1864, Kalischer, together with his longtime associate **Elijah Guttmacher**, founded *Hevrat Yishuv Eretz Yisrael*. Operating initially from their private homes, the organization aimed to raise funds for land acquisition and to establish the infrastructure necessary for agricultural colonies. Despite widespread support in principle, the effort was hampered by limited financial resources and logistical difficulties.

In 1866, recognizing the scale of the undertaking, Kalischer and Guttmacher persuaded the **Alliance Israélite Universelle** to serve as a parent organization. Even with institutional backing, progress remained slow. After years of fundraising, only a modest tract of land could be secured near Jerusalem, with final negotiations completed in the summer of 1874. Kalischer announced the purchase publicly, appealing for donations to complete the final payment. He died two months later, leaving the transaction to be concluded by his family.[29]

THEOLOGICAL REORIENTATION AND MESSIANIC STRATEGY

Kalischer's activism was not driven solely by political developments but also by renewed theological reflection. In the mid-1850s, he revisited rabbinic discussions concerning the restoration of sacrificial worship, reassessing earlier correspondence with authorities such as Akiva Eger and Moses Sofer. This inquiry reinforced his conviction that certain preparatory acts—particularly settlement and agricultural labor—were legitimate and necessary precursors to redemption.

---

[29] On the founding of Mikveh Israel in 1870 and its alignment with Kalischer's settlement vision, see Steele, "Rabbi Kalischer from Toruń."

Over time, Kalischer refined his strategy, concluding that increasing the number of Jews working the land in Palestine was the most practical and theologically defensible immediate objective. Agricultural settlement would, in his view, strengthen Jewish self-sufficiency while aligning with prophetic expectations, without presuming miraculous intervention.

Legacy and Historical Significance

Although Kalischer himself never traveled to Palestine, his influence extended beyond his lifetime. Jewish agricultural initiatives such as **Mikveh Israel**, founded in 1870 near Jaffa, reflected many of the principles he had advocated. His sons and students continued to participate in early settlement movements and proto-Zionist conferences in the decades that followed.

Historians widely regard Kalischer as a foundational figure in the development of religious Zionist thought. Unlike later political Zionists such as **Theodor Herzl**, whose arguments were grounded primarily in modern nationalism, Kalischer's vision remained firmly rooted in covenantal theology and rabbinic tradition. His significance lies in articulating a model of redemption that combined theological fidelity with historical action—an approach that reshaped Jewish messianic discourse in the modern era.

JEWISH OPPOSITION TO ZIONISM AND STATEHOOD

Within Orthodox Judaism, prominent opposition to the Zionist movement and the establishment of the State of Israel came from groups who viewed the return to the Holy Land before the Messiah as a violation of divine will. The most prominent examples are Satmar Hasidism and Neturei Karta.

Satmar Hasidism

The Satmar Movement, one of the largest Hasidic sects in the world, founded by Rabbi Joel Teitelbaum, is strongly anti-Zionist. Its opposition is based on a strict interpretation of the "Three Oaths" found in the Talmud, which forbid Jews from ending the exile by force.

Key theological points:

Satmar theology holds that the two-millennia-long exile was a divine punishment for the sins of the Jewish people.

Therefore, the Jewish people were divinely sworn to wait for a miraculous, messianic redemption and not to return en masse to the land or rebel against the nations of the world by their own human efforts.

The secular, political establishment of the State of Israel is viewed as a blasphemous, human-led usurpation of God's role in the redemption process.

Quotes by Rabbi Joel Teitelbaum:

Rabbi Joel Teitelbaum of Satmar strongly opposed Zionism, calling it a form of spiritual impurity and heresy. He believed the State of Israel hinders redemption, stating, "before the coming of the Messiah, this regime will come to an end." In his book Vayoel Moshe, he declared, "We have no part in Zionism...We'll continue to fight God's war against Zionism."

Neturei Karta

Neturei Karta is an ultra-Orthodox group in Jerusalem that opposes the State of Israel based on the belief that Jews should remain in exile until the Messiah arrives.

Key theological points:

They do not recognize the legitimacy of the state, believing Jewish sovereignty can only be restored by divine intervention.

The ultra-Orthodox see the modern state as a man-made violation of the divine covenant.

Neturei Karta is known for publicly protesting against the state alongside other anti-Israel groups.

Quotes by Rabbi Amram Blau, a founder of Neturei Karta:

Rabbi Amram Blau described Zionism as "counterfeit Judaism," turning the Jewish nation into a secular nationalistic group. He urged Jews to publicly declare they are Jews and "not a Zionist."

Other Orthodox anti-Zionist figures

Rabbi Hayyim Eleazar Shapira: This Hasidic leader saw Zionism as a "renunciation of faith" and a heretical attempt to force the messianic promise.

Rabbi Samson Raphael Hirsch: This 19th-century leader believed promoting emigration to Palestine was a sin, as any human action to bring about the Messiah was considered heretical.

We find then that this "man-made" framework introduced a tension that remains unresolved. If redemption unfolds through ordinary history, how does one distinguish between providence and presumption? At what point does hope become proof? And how does one reconcile prophetic descriptions of cosmic transformation with incremental political progress?

CHRISTIAN PARALLELS

The Gradualization of the Messianic Hope

A remarkably similar shift occurred within Christian prophecy interpretation. Early Christian expectation— shared by the Church Fathers and rooted in apostolic teaching—placed the Messianic Age firmly at the return of Christ. The kingdom would come *with* the King. Judgment, resurrection, and restoration were unified events. Beginning in the nineteenth century, however, new interpretive frameworks emerged that subtly restructured this expectation. Dispensational systems divided prophetic fulfillment into stages, separating physical restoration from spiritual renewal. In this model, Israel could return to the land *before* repentance, *before* Messiah's reign, and *before* judgment—**without contradicting Scripture!**

What the prophets described as a single eschatological act was reimagined as a prolonged sequence. The Messianic Age was no longer the moment when God visibly intervenes, but the final chapter of a process already unfolding through history.

This gradualization had profound implications. If physical restoration could precede spiritual renewal, then political events could be interpreted as prophetic milestones. The presence of Israel in the land became evidence—not of fulfillment completed, but of fulfillment begun.

While Jewish thinkers were promoting *natural redemption,* many Christians were embracing their own version of progressive salvation—what might be called **the theology of gradualism.**

In the nineteenth century, buoyed by scientific progress and imperial confidence, Western theologians increasingly interpreted the kingdom of God as a **social achievement.**

The **Postmillennial** movement taught that through education, moral reform, and missionary expansion, the world would eventually be Christianized, thus inaugurating a millennial era of peace. Christ, in this view, would return *after* the Church had established His kingdom on earth. Sermons and tracts spoke of "redeeming culture" and "bringing in the kingdom" through philanthropy and civilization.

Even in the evangelical sphere, the optimism of progress left its mark. The "Social Gospel" of the late nineteenth century preached that Christianity's mission was to perfect society—to end poverty, war, and injustice—so that Christ's reign might dawn through collective righteousness.

Both **Jewish natural redemption** and **Christian gradualism** shared a crucial presupposition: that the Messianic Age could be *prepared* by human labor. Both replaced the cataclysmic act of God with a cooperative process between heaven and earth. And in both, the transcendent Messiah became secondary to the immanent march of history.

The two traditions moved in opposite directions yet mirrored each other's logic.

- In Jewish thought, **nationhood** preceded Messiah: *return first, redemption later.*

- In Christian gradualism, **morality** preceded Messiah: *reform first, return later.*

93

- Each envisioned the kingdom as the culmination of human progress—a divinely blessed civilization rather than a divinely inaugurated reign.

Isaiah 11 and the Unified Portrait of the Messianic Age

Isaiah's vision in chapter 11 stands as one of the clearest biblical portraits of the Messianic Age. The chapter opens with the Branch from Jesse—a Davidic figure endowed with the Spirit of the LORD—who judges with righteousness and strikes the earth with the rod of His mouth. Wickedness is not managed; it is slain.

Only then does Isaiah speak of restoration. A banner is raised for the nations. The outcasts of Israel are gathered from the four corners of the earth. This gathering is inseparable from the Messiah's reign and the transformation of creation itself.

The famous imagery of peace—wolves dwelling with lambs, children unharmed, violence abolished—does not describe a fragile ceasefire. It describes the end of predation. The earth itself participates in the renewal.

This is the Messianic Age as Scripture presents it: moral, spiritual, political, and cosmic renewal under the visible reign of the Messiah. Any interpretation that isolates one element from the others risks distorting the whole.

By the close of the nineteenth century, expectations once reserved for divine intervention had been recast as historical processes. This shift created a new interpretive problem—one that persists to the present: how to speak of fulfillment without the fulfillment the prophets describe. The next chapter examines the theological consequences of applying prophetic categories prematurely.

Ch. 6: The Problem of Premature Application

The difficulty arises when elements of this vision are applied selectively to modern events. If the gathering of Israel is detached from judgment, repentance, and Messianic rule, it can be redefined as a demographic or political phenomenon. Yet, if peace is postponed, righteousness deferred, and the Messiah absent, the prophetic category is emptied of its defining features.

Two Visions, One Question

Both Jewish natural redemption and Christian gradualist prophecy seek to honor God's promises. Both are motivated by hope rather than hostility. Yet both face the same unresolved question: **can the Messianic Age arrive without the Messiah?**

Having traced these distortions, we must return to the Bible's own definition.

The prophets describe the Messianic Age as the time when:

- The nations beat their swords into plowshares.

- The wolf lies down with the lamb.

- The earth is filled with the knowledge of the Lord.

- Death itself is destroyed.

Each of these conditions requires a transformation of creation—not merely social improvement. Isaiah 2, 11, and 65, together with Micah 4 and Zechariah 14, all depict an age that follows divine judgment and resurrection. It is not inaugurated by human progress but by **divine presence.**

The Messianic Age begins in Scripture not with a vote or a treaty but with an **eruption of holiness**. Isaiah opens his vision with the words, "It shall come to pass in the latter days that the mountain of the Lord's house shall be established on the top of the mountains."[30]

---

[30] Isaiah 2:2.

The imagery is cosmic: God's dwelling rises above every earthly power, and the nations stream toward it. The transformation is moral as well as political—war itself ends because the Judge of all the earth sits enthroned.

Micah, echoing Isaiah, repeats the prophecy almost word for word (Micah 4:1–3), underscoring its centrality in Israel's hope. The "mountain" symbolizes more than geography; it is the elevation of God's righteous rule over every rival claim. The human story does not gradually ascend to this mountain—**the mountain descends upon history**.

The prophets answer decisively. Restoration is not self-authenticating. It does not require interpretation to be recognized. When God gathers His people, judges the nations, renews creation, and reigns in righteousness, the world will know.

THE MARKS OF THE TRUE MESSIANIC AGE

From Genesis to Revelation, the same features reappear:

1. **Divine Intervention** – The Lord Himself descends, judges, and renews.

2. **Universal Peace** – The nations learn war no more; creation is reconciled.

3. **Righteous Rule** – The Messiah governs in person, with justice and omniscience.

4. **Resurrection Life** – Death is overcome; the saints reign with Christ.

5. **Perpetual Presence** – God dwells among His people; separation is ended.

None of these conditions can be accomplished by human progress. All depend upon the direct presence of the Redeemer. The Messianic Age, therefore, cannot be inaugurated by settlement, legislation, or moral reform. It begins only when **He who is the Resurrection and the Life** stands again upon the earth.

A KINGDOM NOT OF THIS WORLD'S MAKING

Jesus told Pilate, "My kingdom is not of this world." He did not mean it would never touch the world, but that it would not arise from its systems. The powers of this age can neither hasten nor hinder its coming. The disciples were told to pray, *"Thy kingdom come,"* but wrong when they asked, "Lord, will You at this time restore the kingdom to Israel?"[31] His answer was not denial but postponement: *"It is not for you to know times or seasons ... but you shall be My witnesses."*

Between His ascension and His return stretches the age of witness—the Church's mission to proclaim the gospel to every nation. The Messianic Age will begin not when the Church succeeds, but when the Son of Man appears in glory.

THE KINGDOM YET TO COME

The biblical portrait is therefore luminous and unmistakable: The Messianic Age is **the reign of Christ on a renewed earth, inaugurated by His appearing, sustained by His presence, and consummated in everlasting peace.**

---

[31] Acts 1:6.

It is not a metaphor for progress but the fulfillment of promise. Every attempt to realize it prematurely—whether through colonization, culture, or creed—mistakes the prelude for the finale.

The prophets saw it from afar; the apostles bore witness to its certainty; the Church awaits it still. When the King returns, the mountain of the Lord will fill the whole earth, and "the knowledge of the glory of the Lord shall cover the earth as the waters cover the sea." (Habakkuk 2:14)

Until that day, the task of faith is not to compress prophecy into current events, but to let Scripture define its own horizon. The Messianic Age remains the goal of history—not merely an early draft.

This distinction prepares us for the next chapter, where we will examine the prophetic language of "gathering" itself—its conditions, its sequence, and its unmistakable signs—to determine whether Scripture allows us to identify that gathering with modern political history, or whether it points us still forward, beyond the limits of human achievement.

The Prophetic Definition

The next section will examine these passages in detail, clarifying what the prophets actually meant by "the last days," "the kingdom of the Lord," and "the reign of peace," and showing how the apostles carried this vision forward into the New Testament expectation of Christ's return.

"Out of Zion shall go forth the law,
and the word of the Lord from Jerusalem.
He shall judge between the nations,
and shall rebuke many people;
they shall beat their swords into plowshares,
and their spears into pruning hooks."
— Isaiah 2:3–4

Isaiah 11 extends this vision by revealing the character of the King who reigns:

"There shall come forth a Rod from the stem of Jesse, and a Branch shall grow out of his roots.
The Spirit of the Lord shall rest upon Him …
With righteousness He shall judge the poor,
and decide with equity for the meek of the earth."
— Isaiah 11:1–4)

The peace that follows—the wolf dwelling with the lamb, the leopard lying down with the kid—signifies not merely political stability but the reconciliation of creation itself. The curse of violence is lifted; predation ceases. Such a transformation cannot be achieved by diplomacy or disarmament. It requires a **new nature**—the renewal Paul later describes when "creation itself will be delivered from the bondage of corruption."[32]

Thus, the Messianic reign is simultaneously **moral, spiritual, and cosmic.** It is not a millennium of improved politics but the restoration of Eden under the rule of the second Adam.

The Lord Himself intervenes, splitting mountains, judging nations, and establishing His universal reign: "And the Lord shall be King over all the earth; in that day it shall be— 'The Lord is one, and His name one.'" (Zechariah 14:9)

The sequence is unmistakable: cataclysm precedes kingdom. The Messianic Age dawns only after divine descent, not before it. Israel's deliverance and the world's renewal coincide in the appearing of her King.

---

[32] Romans 8:21.

The apostles inherit this expectation without dilution. Peter speaks of "the times of restoration of all things" (Acts 3:21)—the very phrase that had stirred the Restorationists centuries later. Yet Peter locates that restoration squarely **after** Christ's return: "whom heaven must receive until the times of restoration." The Messiah reigns presently from heaven, but the earth awaits His revelation.

Paul writes of the same moment in Romans 8:19–23, where creation "groans and labors with birth pangs" until "the revealing of the sons of God." The birth of the new world will not occur through gradual improvement; it comes by divine deliverance.

John's Revelation gives this vision its final shape. After the judgment of Babylon and the coming of Christ as "King of kings and Lord of lords" (Revelation 19:16), the apostle sees the saints reign with Him:

"They lived and reigned with Christ a thousand years … This is the first resurrection." (Revelation 20:4–5)

This reign is the long-awaited **Messianic Kingdom**—a reign that follows resurrection, not precedes it.

105

The millennium of Revelation 20 is not a symbol of slow human progress; it is the display of divine authority after history's consummation. When the final rebellion is crushed, John beholds the ultimate promise:

> "Then I saw a new heaven and a new earth,
> for the first heaven and the first earth had
> passed away." (Revelation 21:1)

Here the Messianic Age merges with eternity; its peace is perpetual, its King visible, its citizens immortal.

Ch. 7: The Prophetic Gathering Examined

THE LANGUAGE OF GATHERING IN THE HEBREW PROPHETS

The idea of Israel's "gathering" stands at the very center of modern prophetic debate. Few biblical terms have been so frequently invoked—and so rarely examined with care. In popular preaching, the word often functions as a self-evident category: Jews returning to the land equals prophetic fulfillment. Yet when the prophetic texts themselves are read in full, the language of gathering proves far more exacting.

The Hebrew prophets do not speak of gathering as a neutral demographic movement. To reiterate, they speak of it as a decisive act of God, bound to judgment, repentance, covenant renewal, and the visible reign of the LORD. To isolate geography from these accompanying features is not interpretation; it is reduction.

Isaiah repeatedly frames the gathering of Israel within a cosmic and moral transformation.

In Isaiah 27:13, the great trumpet is blown, and "those who were lost in the land of Assyria and those who were driven out to the land of Egypt shall come and worship the LORD on the holy mountain at Jerusalem." Worship, not sovereignty, marks the end of exile. The gathering culminates not merely in return, but in restored communion.

Similarly, Isaiah 43:5–7 presents the gathering as an act undertaken directly by God: "I will bring your offspring from the east, and from the west I will gather you… everyone who is called by my name, whom I created for my glory." The stated purpose is not national survival, but divine glory.

Ezekiel's Vision: From Bones to Breath

Perhaps no passage is more frequently cited in discussions of modern Israel than Ezekiel 37. The vision of dry bones coming together has been read by many as a two-stage prophecy: physical restoration first, spiritual restoration later. This reading has become foundational to modern Christian Zionism.

Yet Ezekiel's own interpretation resists such fragmentation. The bones do not merely assemble; they live. Breath enters them. God places His Spirit within them. The vision concludes not with settlement alone, but with covenant restoration: "I will make a covenant of peace with them. It shall be an everlasting covenant" (Ezekiel 37:26).

Ezekiel himself prefaces the vision with divine clarification: "These bones are the whole house of Israel" (37:11). The problem addressed is not statelessness, but hopelessness—"Our hope is lost; we are indeed cut off." The solution is **resurrection**, not **migration**.

As Walther Zimmerli observed in his *Ezekiel* commentary, "The prophet's concern is not political rebirth as such, but the re-creation of Israel as the people of God under Yahweh's sovereign action." This distinction is frequently blurred when the vision is pressed into modern geopolitical service.

Jeremiah and the Moral Conditions of Restoration

Jeremiah's restoration promises are equally stringent. While Jeremiah 31 famously announces a return from exile, it does so in direct connection with the New Covenant: "I will put my law within them, and I will write it on their hearts." The gathering described is inseparable from repentance and internal transformation.

In Jeremiah 30–33, restoration follows "the time of Jacob's trouble," not precedes it. The LORD declares, "I will save you from afar... but I will discipline you in just measure" (Jeremiah 30:10–11). The return is not framed as a political achievement, but as divine deliverance after judgment.

The nineteenth-century theologian Franz Delitzsch warned against treating these passages as incremental: "The restoration spoken of by the prophets is not a piecemeal return effected by human policy, but the final turning of God toward His people in mercy." Such cautions are often absent from contemporary prophecy discourse.

Zechariah and the Day of the LORD

Zechariah brings the prophetic picture to its sharpest focus. Jerusalem's restoration occurs on "the day of the LORD," when the nations are gathered for judgment and the LORD Himself stands on the Mount of Olives (Zechariah 14:3–4). Only after this intervention does the city experience security and holiness.

Zechariah 12–14 leaves little room for ambiguity. Repentance follows divine revelation: "They will look on Me whom they have pierced, and mourn." The gathering of Israel is thus Christological and penitential. It cannot be abstracted from the Messiah without unraveling the prophecy itself.

The Jewish commentator Rashi understood these passages as eschatological, not political. Later rabbinic tradition likewise associated them with the end of days, not with preparatory stages. This continuity of expectation is often overlooked in modern readings.

Jesus and the Timing of the Gathering

The New Testament sharpens the issue rather than resolving it in favor of gradual fulfillment. Jesus places the gathering of the elect *after* tribulation and *after* cosmic signs: "He will send out His angels with a loud trumpet call, and they will **gather** His elect from the four winds" (Matthew 24:31).

The language deliberately echoes Isaiah. Trumpet. Angels. Cosmic disturbance. The gathering is not described as a long historical process but as an eschatological event.

Early Christian interpreters recognized this continuity. Irenaeus wrote that the gathering of Israel would occur "when the Lord shall come from heaven in the clouds, bringing in the times of the kingdom." Augustine, though differing on millennial structure, likewise tied Israel's restoration to Christ's appearing rather than to political arrangements.

THE MODERN REFRAMING OF "GATHERING"

By contrast, modern prophecy teaching often detaches the word "gathering" from its prophetic context. Physical presence in the land becomes sufficient. Moral, spiritual, and Messianic criteria are ignored or postponed.

Hal Lindsey famously wrote, "The rebirth of Israel is the most important prophetic sign of our generation."[33] The assertion is striking not for its confidence, but for its lack of textual controls. The prophets themselves never describe a gathering without repentance, judgment, and divine kingship.

---

[33] Hal Lindsey, *The Late Great Planet Earth* (1970) pp. 53–57.

Jonathan Cahn similarly frames modern events as fulfillments-in-progress, asserting that what we are witnessing is the return foretold by the prophets, even if its fullness lies ahead. Such language depends entirely on the assumption that prophecy may be partially fulfilled in ways the prophets themselves never described.

Criteria, Not Coincidence

The question before us is not whether the Jewish people have returned to the land. They have. Nor is it whether this return is historically remarkable. It is. The question is whether Scripture authorizes us to call this phenomenon the prophetic gathering.

The prophets provide criteria, not impressions. When God gathers Israel, He does so visibly, decisively, and redemptively. Resurrection accompanies return. Repentance accompanies restoration. Messiah accompanies peace. Absent these elements, the gathering remains future—not denied, not diminished, but awaited.

Preparing the Ground for Proof

This chapter has examined the prophetic language of gathering on its own terms. The cumulative testimony of Isaiah, Ezekiel, Jeremiah, Zechariah, and Jesus resists gradualization. The gathering belongs to the Messianic Age itself, not to its prelude.

Having examined the prophetic texts themselves, the question now becomes unavoidable: if Scripture presents the gathering of Israel as a unified, Messiah-centered event, how did the idea of partial fulfillment arise? The answer lies not in the prophets, but in the interpretive frameworks brought to them.

Ch. 8: The Claim of Partial Fulfillment

Once the prophetic criteria for Israel's gathering are taken seriously, a tension emerges that modern interpreters have been reluctant to leave unresolved. On the one hand, the prophets describe a gathering inseparable from repentance, judgment, resurrection, and the visible reign of the Messiah. On the other hand, the twentieth century witnessed the undeniable reconstitution of a Jewish nation in its ancestral land. The pressure to reconcile these two realities has produced what may be called the *partial fulfillment* or *preparatory fulfillment* model.

This model does not usually claim that prophecy has been completed. Instead, it argues that modern Israel represents an initial, incomplete, or preliminary stage of fulfillment—a political restoration that precedes and prepares for a future spiritual consummation. In this view, prophecy is not denied but stretched across time. The gathering has begun, though its meaning has not yet ripened.

At first glance, this approach appears balanced and cautious. It avoids the excesses of date setting while preserving Israel's prophetic significance. Yet its plausibility depends entirely on whether Scripture itself recognizes such a category. The question is not whether partial fulfillment is *convenient*, but whether it is *biblical*.

DISPENSATIONAL ROOTS OF THE TWO-STAGE GATHERING

The partial-fulfillment framework did not arise organically from the prophetic texts. It arose from nineteenth-century dispensational theology, which divided redemptive history into discrete administrations and sharply distinguished Israel from the Church. Within this system, promises to Israel could be fulfilled literally, politically, and nationally— while still awaiting a later spiritual completion.

C. I. Scofield expressed this logic succinctly in his notes on Ezekiel, arguing that Israel's restoration would occur:

"**in unbelief** first, and afterward in faith."

This assumption—rarely argued from the text itself—became foundational. The presence of Israel in the land was sufficient to qualify as fulfillment, even if the covenantal conditions described by the prophets remained unmet.

Lewis Sperry Chafer, founder of Dallas Theological Seminary, reinforced this view, writing that Israel's regathering would be "a national restoration apart from spiritual regeneration," which would come only after the Church age concluded. The prophetic sequence was thus reversed: geography first, repentance later.

What is striking is that this sequencing is not drawn from Isaiah, Jeremiah, Ezekiel, or Zechariah, but imposed upon them. The prophets consistently move from judgment to repentance to restoration, not from restoration to repentance.

Jewish Parallels: Natural Redemption Revisited

As noted earlier, a similar structure appears in modern Jewish religious Zionism. Rabbi Abraham Isaac Kook taught that secular Zionist activity, though outwardly irreligious, constituted the early phase of divine redemption. The return to the land was itself redemptive, even if the people had not yet returned to God.

Kook famously described the pioneers of Zionism as "unknowing agents of redemption," instruments through whom God advanced His purposes without their conscious faith. In this framework, moral and spiritual renewal would follow national revival rather than precede it.

The parallel with Christian partial-fulfillment theology is unmistakable. In both cases, prophecy is divided into manageable stages, allowing history to shoulder the weight of fulfillment before heaven intervenes. Redemption becomes a process rather than an event.

Yet traditional Jewish critics of religious Zionism warned that this approach blurred the line between providence and presumption. Rabbi Joel Teitelbaum, the Satmar Rebbe, argued vehemently that political sovereignty achieved before the Messiah constituted a violation of divine order. In his view, redemption without repentance was not partial—it was counterfeit.

The Absence of a Biblical Category

The central difficulty with the partial-fulfillment model is not that it is ill-intentioned, but that it lacks clear biblical precedent. Scripture does recognize *types* and *foreshadows*, but these do not function as partial fulfillments of the same prophecy. A type points forward; it does not begin the event it anticipates.

When Old Testament prophecies are fulfilled in the New Testament, they are fulfilled decisively. The suffering servant does not partially atone. The resurrection does not begin gradually. Pentecost is not the early phase of the Spirit's outpouring—it is the outpouring.

N. T. Wright, though not aligned with dispensational theology, nonetheless cautions against "stretching prophetic language across unrelated historical events in order to preserve theological expectations." Prophecy, he argues, must be allowed to define its own fulfillment, rather than be retrofitted to history.

The prophets do not speak of Israel being gathered *in unbelief*. They speak of Israel being gathered *because unbelief has been healed*. The causal direction matters.

MATTHEW 24 AND THE PROBLEM OF TIMING

Jesus' own teaching presents a decisive challenge to the partial-fulfillment claim. In the Olivet Discourse, He places the gathering of the elect after tribulation and cosmic disturbance, not before. "Immediately after the tribulation of those days," He says, "He will send out His angels… and they will gather His elect" (Matthew 24:29–31).

Here's where we'll look to the Olivet Discourse in Matthew Chapter 24 (also in Luke 21). The Disciples had asked Jesus a two-part question about: 1) When the Second Temple would be destroyed, and, 2) What would be the sign of Jesus' Second Coming and the end of the age?

In verses 4-8, Jesus gives the Beginning of Sorrows (or Birth Pains). These are presented as general tribulations throughout the age.

We see:

- Religious deception
- Wars and rumors of wars
- Famines and earthquakes in various places

- •   Persecution of believers
- •   The rise of false prophets
- •   And an increase of lawlessness

But then, Jesus gives some specific events:

- •   The gospel is preached to all nations
- •   Abomination of desolation—spoken of by Daniel

We'll come back to the Abomination. First, let's move down to verse 21.

> "For then there will be great tribulation, such as has not been since the beginning of the world until this time, no, nor ever shall be."

And here this Greek word for world is *Kosmos*, so it's talking about the Planet.

This event is the elephant in the room. If you believe in a Young Earth, this "great tribulation" will be more devastating than Noah's Flood. If you believe in a recently inhabited Old Earth, this will be worse than the Chicxulub asteroid impact.[34]

---

[34] According to geological dating, approximately 66 million years ago, a massive asteroid impact at Chicxulub on

In fact, Jesus said, without intervention, "no flesh would survive," clearly classifying this tribulation as an extinction level event. When we look at the next verse (29), and correlative passages throughout the Bible, this great tribulation most closely resembles an asteroid strike.

> "Immediately after the tribulation of those days the sun will be darkened, and the moon will not give its light; the stars will fall from heaven, and the powers of the heavens will be shaken."

Revelation says, "The stars of the sky fell to the earth, as the fig tree sheds its winter fruit when shaken by a gale..." "Something like a great mountain, burning with fire, was thrown into the sea..."

Isaiah 24 says, "The earth staggers like a drunkard; it sways like a hut in the wind." That would seem to indicate the Earth's spin or axis has changed.

But no one will miss this ultimate geo/astrological catastrophe.

Mexico's Yucatán Peninsula triggered the Cretaceous-Paleogene (K-Pg) mass extinction, ending the reign of the dinosaurs.

Verse 30: (And now, this is where Jesus gives the Disciples that sign they had asked for):

> "Then the sign of the Son of Man will appear in heaven, and then all the tribes of the earth will mourn, and they will see the Son of Man coming on the clouds of heaven with power and great glory."

This is where Luke 21 tells us to "lift your heads for your redemption draws nigh." Verse 31:

> "And He will send His angels with a great sound of a trumpet, and they will gather together His chosen ones from the four winds, from one end of heaven to the other."

Verse 31 makes it crystal-clear, that the biblical **gathering of Israel** occurs **after** Jesus returns. Which comes **after** that blowout event.

Verse 33 Says, when you see "*all these things*."

THE FIG TREE IN PERSPECTIVE TO CATACLYSM

Next, Jesus gives the parable of the fig tree.

But Jesus **doesn't** say, "When you see this very last thing I mentioned!" He says when you see *all these things,*—which includes that ultimate calamity.

In verse 34, Jesus says, "This generation shall not pass away till **all these things**" take place. Again, *all these things*. (Revelation 13 says that during this overlapping interval of time, "*No one* will be able to buy or sell without the mark of the beast.")

So *no one* is going to survive long after the greatest disaster in the history of the world! Jesus says they won't make it past one generation.

Bible prophecy timers typically add 70 to 80 years onto the date of some specific event—say, for instance like 1948 or 1967...

But the way to calculate when Jesus is coming is simply to subtract the 70 to 80 years of a generation from the date of Verse Twenty-one's mega disaster. But wait! No one can do that. And that's what Jesus says in verse 36,

"But of that day and hour no one knows…"

So when someone throws out some date,—as listed at the beginning of this book—they're saying they know for certain when that asteroid, or eruption or whatever it is, will occur—within the margin of error of one generation.

Notice again, that a fig tree is not in the list of *all these things* before Jesus returns.

It's an example. Luke says, "The fig tree and all the trees, when *they* are already budding." The obvious meaning is that we should observe the process of how fruit trees work.

To hammer home the fact that there is no surefire-preceding-sign (such as a fig tree), Jesus references the unpredictability of Noah's Flood.

> "But no one knows of that day and hour, not even the angels of heaven, but my Father only. As the days of Noah were, so will the coming of the Son of Man be. For as in those days which were before the flood they were eating and drinking, marrying and giving in marriage, until the day that Noah entered into the ship, and they didn't know until the flood came and took them all away, **so will the coming of the Son of Man be**." vs. 36-39.

Now, the abomination of desolation *is* on that list of *all these things*. The early church looked to 2nd Thessalonians 2 for "the one restraining" and "the Son of Perdition" who is associated with the abomination of desolation.

But they expected the abomination to come in a spiritual sense; in line with 1st Peter 2 and Ephesians 2, where the Church is built up into a spiritual temple. For those trained in Dispensational Theology or otherwise schooled in pre-tribulation rapture teaching, it may come as a surprise that the 1982 New King James Version was the first major English Bible to capitalize the pronoun "He" in 2 Thessalonians 2:7, suggesting that the Holy Spirit is the restrainer and the one taken out of the way. Even the editors of Scofield's Reference Bible didn't take the liberty to capitalize these pronouns.

The verse reads:

> "For the mystery of lawlessness is already at work. Only he who now restrains it, will do so until he is taken out of the way."

These pronouns aren't capitalized in the Greek. There is no way of knowing the antecedents of these pronouns because Paul is asking the Thessalonians to remember something he had told them before. We don't even know if the one restraining is the same "he" as the "he" that is "taken out of the way."

Up through the 6th century, the Early Church Fathers,—Tertullian, John Chrysostom, Jerome, and Augustine—all wrote that the Roman Empire was the one restraining lawlessness.

Then, the Protestant Reformers equated the one-thousand-two-hundred and sixty days in prophecy with the 1260 years that the Holy Roman Empire had been restraining the papacy, which they saw as the Antichrist.

If this gathering has already begun in 1948, then Jesus' Matthew 24 chronology collapses. The "sign" He names—darkened sun, shaken powers of heaven, the visible appearance of the Son of Man—have not occurred. The partial-fulfillment model thus requires the gathering to occur without the very specific sign Jesus told the disciples to look for.

The Elasticity of Proof

Once partial fulfillment is admitted, prophecy loses its capacity to falsify interpretations. Any development can be declared significant without ever being decisive. When expectations fail, fulfillment is simply deferred. What was once imminent becomes ongoing. What was once proof becomes potential.

This elasticity explains why failed timetables rarely discredit the underlying system. If fulfillment is always partial, it is never wrong—only incomplete.

Karl Barth warned against this very move when he cautioned that prophecy must not be converted into "a wax nose, to be bent in any direction history requires." Though Barth wrote from a different theological tradition, his warning applies with equal force here.

History without a Verdict

To say that modern Israel is historically extraordinary is incontestable. To say that it is morally complex is unavoidable. But to say that it constitutes partial prophetic fulfillment is a claim Scripture itself does not clearly authorize.

The prophets did not offer fragments of redemption to be assembled over centuries. They proclaimed a day when God would act, vindicate His name, and restore His people unmistakably. Until that day arrives, history remains history—remarkable, tragic, hopeful, but not yet eschatological.

The Question That Remains

If the Bible does not recognize a category of partial gathering, what then are we to make of modern Israel? That question cannot be answered by denial or enthusiasm alone. It requires us to distinguish carefully between providence and prophecy, between historical survival and eschatological restoration. The next chapter will take up that task by examining Israel's modern return on its own historical terms—without prematurely assigning it a prophetic verdict.

Only then can we ask, with intellectual honesty and biblical fidelity, what modern Israel proves,—and what it does not.

Ch. 9: The Modern Return Examined Historically

H If the modern return of the Jewish people to the land is to be evaluated honestly, it must first be examined on its own historical terms. To begin with prophecy and then search history for confirmation is to reverse the proper order of inquiry. Scripture itself never instructs the reader to baptize political events as fulfillment; it provides criteria by which fulfillment may later be recognized.

This chapter therefore approaches the modern return without assigning it a prophetic verdict. It asks a narrower, more disciplined question: *What actually happened?* Only after history is allowed to speak plainly can theology be responsibly applied.

Early Zionism: A Secular National Project

Contrary to popular imagination, political Zionism did not arise as a religious revival movement. Its earliest architects were overwhelmingly secular, and in many cases explicitly anti-religious.

131

Theodor Herzl, often called the father of modern Zionism, did not ground his vision in prophecy but in political necessity. In *Der Judenstaat* (1896), Herzl argued that antisemitism was an ineradicable feature of European society and that Jewish safety required sovereignty.

Herzl's proposal was pragmatic rather than theological. He initially considered locations other than Palestine, including Argentina and Uganda. The land of Israel was chosen not because prophecy demanded it, but because history, symbolism, and international diplomacy made it viable. Zionism, at its inception, was a nationalist response to European failure, not a messianic movement.

This fact troubled many religious Jews. Traditional rabbinic authorities rejected political Zionism precisely because it severed return from repentance and redemption from Messiah. The divide between secular Zionists and religious opponents would persist for decades and has never fully healed.

The Balfour Declaration and Imperial Interests

The modern return accelerated not through spontaneous migration alone, but through the intervention of imperial powers. The Balfour Declaration of 1917, issued by the British government, expressed support for "the establishment in Palestine of a national home for the Jewish people." The declaration was not a theological statement. It emerged from a convergence of wartime strategy, colonial calculation, and Restorationist sympathy among British elites. Britain sought influence in the eastern Mediterranean, support among Jewish communities, and stability in a collapsing Ottoman region.

Importantly, the declaration also promised, "nothing shall be done which may prejudice the civil and religious rights of existing non-Jewish communities in Palestine." This unresolved tension—between Jewish national aspirations and Arab population realities—would define the conflict that followed.

Mandate, Migration, and Conflict

Under the British Mandate (1920–1948), Jewish immigration increased steadily. Some immigrants were motivated by idealism, others by desperation as antisemitism intensified across Europe. Land purchases, agricultural settlements, and new institutions transformed the demographic landscape.

At the same time, Arab resistance grew. Riots, strikes, and revolts reflected fears of displacement and loss of self-determination. British authorities oscillated between encouraging Zionist development and attempting to placate Arab opposition through restrictive White Papers.

By the late 1930s, the situation had become untenable. Europe stood on the brink of catastrophe. The Holocaust would soon erase any remaining doubt about the vulnerability of Jewish life without a refuge.

1948: Statehood through War

The declaration of the State of Israel in May 1948 was not the climax of prophetic expectation, but the outcome of political process followed by military conflict. The United Nations partition plan of 1947 was rejected by Arab leaders and accepted by Jewish representatives. War followed immediately.

Israel's survival in the 1948 Arab–Israeli War was remarkable, but it was not miraculous in the biblical sense. It involved organization, strategy, external support, and costly sacrifice. Hundreds of thousands of Palestinians were displaced in what they call the *Nakba* ("catastrophe"), embedding a humanitarian crisis into the foundation of the state.

These realities do not invalidate Israel's existence, but they complicate any attempt to frame its birth as a purely redemptive act. The prophets describe a restoration without injustice; history delivered statehood through conflict.

THE CHARACTER OF THE NEW STATE

The State of Israel that emerged was consciously secular. Its founders did not proclaim the reign of Messiah, the renewal of covenant, or national repentance. The Declaration of Independence invokes the "Rock of Israel," a phrase deliberately ambiguous enough to accommodate both believers and atheists.

Hebrew was revived, institutions built, borders defended. But the defining features of prophetic restoration—resurrection, righteousness, peace among the nations, universal knowledge of God—were absent.

David Ben-Gurion himself stated that the Bible was Israel's "mandate," but not its constitution. The state was to be governed by human law, not divine revelation. This distinction matters profoundly for prophetic interpretation.

Survival, Not Salvation

Israel's continued survival through successive wars—in 1956, 1967, 1973, and beyond—has often been cited as evidence of divine favor. Survival, however, is not synonymous with redemption. Many nations have endured against odds without claiming prophetic fulfillment.

The Six-Day War of 1967, in which Israel gained control of Jerusalem's Old City, intensified prophetic speculation. Yet even here, the prophetic markers remained absent. No repentance followed. No messianic reign commenced. The nations were not judged; they were realigned.

History again proved elastic enough to sustain multiple interpretations, but Scripture remained specific.

Providence without Fulfillment

None of this requires a denial of God's providence. Scripture affirms that God governs the rise and fall of nations. Cyrus of Persia was called God's "anointed" without being a redeemer. Rome was used to accomplish divine purposes without being the kingdom of God.

To say that God permitted, guided, or even used the modern return does not require us to identify it as prophetic fulfillment. Providence explains *how* events occur; prophecy explains *what* God has promised to do.

Confusing the two invites theological inflation— treating history as eschatology simply because it is extraordinary.

History's Proper Weight

The modern return of Israel is one of the most consequential political developments of the twentieth century. It deserves careful historical understanding, moral seriousness, and sober reflection. But history alone cannot certify prophecy.

Only when the Messiah reigns, the nations are judged, the dead are raised, and the knowledge of the LORD covers the earth will the prophets' words be fulfilled in their fullness.

Until then, modern Israel remains what history shows it to be, a nation reborn through human struggle, sustained by resilience, marked by conflict, and surrounded by unresolved questions.

In the chapters that follow, we will examine how the prophets envision the culmination of this covenant story, and how modern claims of fulfillment measure against those visions. But before prophecy can be assessed, the people to whom the promises were given must be rightly understood.

Ch. 10: The People of the Covenant

Few questions have generated more theological confusion—or more political heat—than the question of *who* constitutes the people of God. Is covenant identity determined by bloodline or by belief, or somehow by both/and? Is the criterion by historical election or present faithfulness; by divine promise or human response to the promise? These questions are not academic abstractions. They shape how Scripture is read, how prophecy is interpreted, and how modern Israel is understood in relation to biblical expectation.

At the heart of the debate lies a basic tension within the biblical narrative itself: Israel is unmistakably a *chosen people*, yet the Scriptures repeatedly warn that covenant privilege does not guarantee covenant faithfulness. From the earliest chapters of the Torah to the latest writings of the apostles, the people of God are defined not merely by descent, but by relationship—by hearing, receiving, and responding to the word of the Lord.

COVENANT BEFORE NATION

The story of Israel begins not with a nation, but with a promise. Abram is called out of Mesopotamia before he has land, descendants, or political identity. The covenant precedes the people; the people do not create the covenant. "I will make of you a great nation," God declares, binding the future of Abram's offspring to divine initiative rather than human achievement.

This ordering matters. Israel is not chosen because it exists; it exists because it is chosen. The covenant establishes Israel's identity before Israel becomes Israel in any sociological sense. Even circumcision, the covenant sign, is given after the promise, not as its cause but as its seal.

Later biblical writers return to this priority again and again. Moses reminds the people that their election was not based on numerical strength or moral superiority. The prophets insist that possession of covenant markers—Temple, land, lineage—does not immunize Israel from judgment. Yet, covenant relationship, not covenant symbolism, is decisive.

A Corporate Identity with Moral Conditions

At Sinai, Israel becomes a nation in the fullest sense: bound by law, organized under divine kingship, and charged with a representative vocation. "You shall be to me a kingdom of priests and a holy nation." The language is corporate and collective, but it is never unconditional in the sense of moral automatism.

The covenant includes blessings and curses, life and death set before the people. Fidelity matters. Obedience matters. Repentance matters. This does not negate divine faithfulness; it clarifies human responsibility within a covenantal framework.

The exile exposes this tension dramatically. Israel remains God's people even in judgment, yet the loss of land and Temple demonstrates that covenant status does not eliminate historical consequence. The prophets speak of a remnant—faithful within the unfaithful—preserved by grace but refined by discipline. The people of the covenant are thus both broader than any momentary political structure but narrower than ethnic totality.

The Remnant Principle

The concept of a remnant is not an innovation of later theology; it is woven into the fabric of Israel's Scriptures. God preserves a faithful core through whom His purposes continue, even when the majority falters. The remnant remains Israel, not a replacement for Israel. Yet it also demonstrates that covenant participation is relational, not mechanical. One can belong to Israel and yet be cut off; one can be cut down and yet restored. The covenant people are real, historical, and embodied—but also spiritually accountable.

This remnant logic becomes crucial for understanding how the New Testament speaks about Israel without abandoning the Old Testament's categories.

MESSIAH AND THE COVENANT PEOPLE

The arrival of Jesus intensifies, rather than dissolves, the covenant question. He comes explicitly "to the lost sheep of the house of Israel," announcing the nearness of the kingdom promised by the prophets. His ministry is saturated with covenant imagery: twelve disciples echoing the twelve tribes, Passover reinterpreted, Temple symbolism fulfilled and transcended.

Yet Jesus also introduces a decisive criterion: allegiance to himself as the Messiah. Faithfulness to the covenant is now inseparable from response to the One in whom the covenant's promises converge. Jesus warned the Jews of Jerusalem, "Unless you believe that I AM, you will die in your sins."[35] The earliest Jesus-followers do not imagine themselves founding a new religion detached from Israel's story. They understand themselves as Jews who have recognized Israel's Messiah. The controversy arises not because the covenant is discarded, but because its fulfillment is contested.

Inclusion without Erasure

The inclusion of Gentiles presents the most explosive covenant question of the early church. Can those outside Israel's ethnic boundaries participate in Israel's promises? The apostolic answer is a qualified but emphatic yes—without requiring Gentiles to become Jews in a national or ceremonial sense.

---

[35] John 8:24.

This inclusion is framed not as replacement but as participation. Gentiles are grafted in, brought near, made fellow heirs.

> Ephesians 2:11-21 (WEB) "Therefore remember that once you, the Gentiles in the flesh, who are called 'uncircumcision' by that which is called 'circumcision' (in the flesh, made by hands), that you were at that time separate from Christ, alienated from the commonwealth of Israel, and strangers from the covenants of the promise, having no hope and without God in the world. But now in Christ Jesus you who once were far off are made near in the blood of Christ. For he is our peace, who made both one, and broke down the middle wall of separation, having abolished in his flesh the hostility, the law of commandments contained in ordinances, that he might create in himself one new man of the two, making peace, and might reconcile them both in one body to God through the cross, having killed the hostility through it. He came and preached peace to you who were far off and to those who were near. For through him we both have our access in one Spirit to the Father. So then you are no longer strangers and foreigners, but you are fellow

citizens with the saints and of the household of God, being built on the foundation of the apostles and prophets, Christ Jesus himself being the chief cornerstone; in whom the whole building, fitted together, grows into a holy temple in the Lord; in whom you also are built together for a habitation of God in the Spirit."

PAUL'S MYSTERY OF ISRAEL'S FULLNESS

In Romans 11, Paul confronts the enigma of Israel's partial unbelief.

He sees in it both tragedy and purpose:

> "Through their fall salvation has come to the Gentiles, to provoke them to jealousy." (Verse 11)

But he also foresees a day of reversal:

> "If their being cast away is the reconciling of the world, what will their acceptance be but life from the dead?" (Verse 15)

This "life from the dead" echoes the resurrection theme of Ezekiel 37—it is the *second breath*, the spiritual revival of a nation reconciled to her Messiah. Paul concludes with that glorious assurance:

"And so all Israel will be saved." (Verse 26)

This salvation is not achieved by diplomacy or demography; it comes when "the Deliverer will come out of Zion."

In that moment, the physical and the spiritual, the earthly and the heavenly, converge. Israel's acceptance becomes the world's renewal; the restoration of one people becomes the resurrection of all.

In Romans 11:17-24, the Nations (Gentiles) are *added to* Ephesians' "household of God."

> "But if some of the branches were broken off, and you, being a wild olive, were grafted in among them and became partaker with them of the root and of the richness of the olive tree, don't boast over the branches. But if you boast, remember that it is not you who support the root, but the root supports you. You will say then, 'Branches were broken off, that I might be grafted in.' True; by their unbelief they were broken off, and you stand by your faith. Don't be conceited, but fear; for if God didn't spare the natural branches,

neither will he spare you. See then the goodness and severity of God. Toward those who fell, severity; but toward you, goodness, if you continue in his goodness; otherwise you also will be cut off. They also, if they don't continue in their unbelief, will be grafted in, for God is able to graft them in again. For if you were cut out of that which is by nature a wild olive tree, and were grafted contrary to nature into a good olive tree, how much more will these, which are the natural branches, be grafted into their own olive tree?"

Yet the metaphors consistently preserve Israel's priority and identity. The root remains. The promises remain. The warnings against arrogance remain as well.

The covenant people are thus expanded, not redefined or omitted:

"Indeed, he says, 'It is too light a thing that you should be my servant to raise up the tribes of Jacob, and to restore the preserved of Israel. I will also give you as a light to the nations, that you may be my salvation to the end of the earth'" Isaiah 49:6.

Faith becomes the means of participation, but the story into which faith enters remains Israel's story.

Modern Confusions

Much contemporary debate about Israel falters by flattening these distinctions. On one side, covenant identity is collapsed into modern political sovereignty, as though statehood itself constituted fulfillment. On the other, Israel is spiritualized into insignificance, absorbed entirely into a generic church identity with no ongoing historical particularity.

Both moves distort the biblical witness. Scripture refuses to reduce the people of the covenant either to a mere nation-state or to a purely spiritual idea. Israel is a people with a history, a calling, a discipline, and a future shaped by divine promise and human response.

Recognizing this complexity does not answer every prophetic question—but it does establish necessary guardrails. Any claim about Israel's role in the present must account for covenant continuity, moral accountability, messianic fulfillment, and unresolved expectation.

THE COVENANT STILL SPEAKS

The people of the covenant are not an artifact of ancient history. They remain central to the biblical narrative precisely because the covenant itself remains operative. God has not abandoned His purposes, nor has He simplified them for modern convenience.

> "For the gifts and the calling of God are irrevocable. For as you in time past were disobedient to God, but now have obtained mercy by their disobedience, even so these also have now been disobedient, that by the mercy shown to you they may also obtain mercy. For God has bound all to disobedience, that he might have mercy on all" Romans 11:29-32.

Israel's story is still unfolding, not as a blank check for political action, nor as a discarded chapter in salvation history, but as a living testimony to the faithfulness of God amid human failure. To speak of Israel is therefore to speak of covenant—serious, demanding, gracious, and unfinished.

Ch. 11: The Proof in the Prophets

"He who scattered Israel will gather him,
and keep him as a shepherd does his flock."
— Jeremiah 31:10

If covenant defines the people, then prophecy defines the outcome. No claim about Israel—ancient or modern—can be sustained apart from the prophetic witness, for it is the prophets who interpret Israel's past, diagnose her present, and announce her future. They do not speak in fragments or contradictions. Across centuries and circumstances, a single, coherent pattern governs every promise of Israel's restoration.

That pattern is neither gradual nor ambiguous. From Moses to Malachi, and echoed again by Christ and the apostles, the prophetic sequence unfolds in a consistent order:

- Israel is scattered in judgment.
- Israel repents and is renewed in heart.
- God intervenes decisively—not through human enterprise.
- Israel is gathered and raised.
- The Messiah reigns in righteousness and peace.

151

Every prophet follows this order. None reverse it. None omit its moral or messianic center. And none locate the decisive gathering in the ordinary course of history. The restoration of Israel belongs to the climax of redemptive history, not to its slow, political unfolding.

What follows is not a selective proof-texting exercise, but a cumulative survey of the major prophetic witnesses, arranged so their shared testimony can be heard in full.

THE FOUNDATIONAL PROMISE: MOSES AND THE END IN VIEW

The prophetic story begins, fittingly, with Moses. Long before Israel entered the land, Moses declared that exile would follow disobedience—but exile would not be the final word. In Deuteronomy 30, he describes a future moment when Israel, scattered among the nations, would come to repentance:

"Then the Lord your God will bring you back from captivity, and have compassion on you, and gather you again from all the nations where He has scattered you."

The gathering Moses envisions is universal—"from the farthest parts under heaven"—and transformative. God Himself circumcises Israel's heart, enabling covenant obedience. Restoration is therefore neither automatic nor political. It is moral and miraculous: repentance first, divine action second.

This foundational structure governs everything that follows. Any later "return" that bypasses repentance or depends primarily on human initiative fails Moses' own test.

ISAIAH AND THE SECOND EXODUS

Isaiah expands Moses' promise into a global vision. In Isaiah 11, the restoration of Israel occurs "the second time," echoing the Exodus but surpassing it in scope. The remnant is recovered not merely from Babylon, but from Assyria, Egypt, Cush, Elam, and "the islands of the sea."

Crucially, this gathering follows the revelation of the "Root of Jesse." The nations seek Him. Universal peace prevails. The earth is filled with the knowledge of the Lord.

Isaiah does not describe a preparatory stage of human-led return. He describes a messianic age inaugurated by divine rule. The restoration of Israel is inseparable from the reign of the Messiah.

Later, Isaiah sharpens this expectation with the image of the "great trumpet," blown on a single day, summoning the scattered sons of Israel. The language anticipates resurrection, not relocation. Jesus Himself would later echo this imagery when speaking of the gathering of the elect at the end of the age.

JEREMIAH: THE BRANCH, THE COVENANT, AND COSMIC PERMANENCE

Jeremiah speaks into national collapse with uncompromising clarity. God Himself scattered Israel; God Himself will regather her. But this gathering occurs under the reign of a "righteous Branch," a king who executes justice and righteousness in the land.

Jeremiah refuses to separate restoration from kingship. The people are gathered *because* the Lord reigns. The **Shepherd** and the **flock** appear together.

In Jeremiah 31, this same moment is identified with the New Covenant. Israel is forgiven, inwardly transformed, and restored—not merely to land, but to relationship. Lest anyone imagine this covenant nullifies Israel's identity, Jeremiah anchors it to the permanence of the created order. Only if the sun and stars fail will Israel cease to be a nation before God.

History has known partial returns. It has never known the conditions Jeremiah describes.

EZEKIEL: FROM PRESERVATION TO RESURRECTION

Ezekiel's testimony is among the most explicit and most abused. Writing from exile, he describes two inseparable movements: cleansing and resurrection. In Ezekiel 36, Israel is regathered for God's own name's sake, washed, given a new heart, and filled with the Spirit. In chapter 37, the famous vision of dry bones dramatizes the same truth. The bones come together first—structure without life. Only afterward does breath enter.

The sequence is decisive. Physical preservation precedes spiritual resurrection, but resurrection is the goal. The prophecy concludes with a reunited Israel under "David My servant" forever, an everlasting covenant, and a permanent sanctuary.

155

No merely temporal restoration can satisfy such language. Such unity is only realized now on a spiritual level as the Household of God of Ephesians 2, and the "grafted in" unity of Romans 11. This spiritual gathering *has* occurred so that "There is neither Jew nor Gentile, neither slave nor free, nor is there male and female, for you are all one in Christ Jesus." But Galatians 3:28 addresses Jews who also believe in Jesus; and speaks on personal rather than national terms.

HOSEA, JOEL, AND THE LATTER DAYS

Hosea compresses Israel's long exile into a single sentence: "many days" without king or sacrifice. The return comes "afterward," in "the latter days," when Israel seeks both the Lord and "David their king." The defining mark of restoration is messianic recognition.

Joel reinforces the same sequence: repentance, outpouring of the Spirit, cosmic signs, and then gathering and judgment. The Spirit who awakens repentance also heralds the day of the Lord. Restoration and reckoning arrive together.

Amos speaks of the rebuilding of David's fallen tabernacle—a prophecy James later cites to explain the inclusion of the Gentiles in Christ. Yet Amos' final promise extends beyond present history: Israel is planted in the land "never again to be uprooted." Only the new creation can fulfill such eternal permanence.

Micah echoes Isaiah's vision of Zion exalted, nations streaming, and the Lord reigning forever. Deliverance from captivity and dominion under the King occur in the same divine act.

Zechariah presents the most explicit convergence of prophecy. Israel looks upon the One she pierced. A fountain for cleansing is opened. The Lord's feet stand on the Mount of Olives. National repentance, divine revelation, and the physical return of the King unfold together.

The Branch in Zechariah
and the Messianic Temple

In Zechariah 6, the prophecy concerning the "Branch" is a messianic vision of a coming figure who would rebuild the Temple. However, it is a spiritual, not a physical, temple, and most biblical scholars assess it as being administered by the Messiah through the cross or upon his return.

The Branch as Messiah

A priest on his throne: Zechariah 6:12–13 states that the Branch "shall build the temple of the Lord" and "shall be a priest on his throne," indicating a merging of the offices of king and high priest in one person.

Messianic title: The title "the Branch" (Hebrew: Tsemach) was a well-known messianic designation in the Old Testament, used by prophets like Isaiah and Jeremiah. This makes the figure of the Branch, a "man whose name is the Branch," a clear reference to the Messiah.

A spiritual temple: The "temple of the Lord" he builds is not the physical one being rebuilt by Zerubbabel at the time, but the eschatological and spiritual temple associated with the Messiah's coming. In Christian theology, this refers to the Church, which consists of believers as "living stones," with Christ as the chief cornerstone.

The Second Coming and the Branch's Temple

There are varying interpretations concerning the Branch's temple and how it relates to the Second Coming. Reigning and building: Some views connect the Branch's building of the Temple to the inauguration of his reign at his first advent, viewing the Church as the temple being built during the present age. This reflects an amillennial or covenant premillennial view.

Millennial temple: Other interpretations suggest the Branch will build a literal millennial Temple upon his return. Proponents of this view see the Branch's work as a future event, fulfilling prophecies related to the Millennium.

Zechariah's Temple and Ezekiel's Temple

The vision of the Temple in Zechariah relates to the Third Temple described by Ezekiel, but they are not identical.

Ezekiel's symbolic vision: Many biblical scholars see Ezekiel's detailed description (Ezekiel 40-48) as symbolic and not meant to be a literal blueprint for a physical structure. This vision emphasizes the return of God's glory to a restored Jerusalem, depicting the ideal community and world to come rather than a physical temple.

Ideal vs. physical: The discrepancies between Ezekiel's vision and the Second Temple, which the exiles actually built, suggest that Ezekiel's vision described a future, more perfect fulfillment.

Overlap in fulfillment: The Branch of Zechariah and the Temple of Ezekiel both point to the restoration of God's presence among his people. While the Branch's building project is primarily spiritual (the Church), Ezekiel's vision presents a vivid image of God's presence in the Eschaton.

Synthesis of Zechariah and Ezekiel

The different interpretations of Zechariah and Ezekiel on the Third Temple reflect variations in eschatological beliefs, particularly regarding how prophecies about a restored Israel and a new Temple are fulfilled.

Christ's finished work: Some theological perspectives argue that Christ's finished work has fulfilled the need for an earthly temple and sacrificial system. They view the Church as the fulfillment of the Temple prophecies. From this standpoint, the idea of a literal Third Temple with sacrifices would be a backward step in redemptive history.

Inaugurated eschatology: Other views see an initial fulfillment in Christ's first coming and the spiritual Temple of the Church, with a literal, final fulfillment upon his Second Coming. This perspective allows for both spiritual and physical realities to be addressed by the prophecies.

The tension between Zechariah's spiritual Temple and Ezekiel's more detailed, literal-sounding description is ultimately resolved in eschatology, with a view toward Christ's ultimate work, which will encompass the whole of creation and bring about the final and perfect dwelling place of God with humanity. Daniel places Israel's final deliverance after an unparalleled time of trouble and explicitly links it to resurrection. Deliverance and awakening occur simultaneously. No interpretation confined to modern politics can absorb such realities.

161

The New Testament does not revise this prophetic structure; it confirms it. Jesus speaks of the gathering of the elect *after* the tribulation. Paul locates Israel's salvation at the coming of the Deliverer out of Zion. Revelation places restoration beyond judgment, beyond war, beyond death itself.

The apostles do not announce the completion of Israel's prophetic hope. They announce its nearness.

2nd Thessalonians 2:1-4 Now concerning the coming of our Lord Jesus Christ and our being **gathered** together to him, we ask you, brothers, not to be quickly shaken in mind or alarmed, either by a spirit or a spoken word, or a letter seeming to be from us, to the effect that the day of the Lord has come. Let no one deceive you in any way. For that day will not come, unless the rebellion comes first, and the man of lawlessness is revealed, the son of destruction, who opposes and exalts himself against every so-called god or object of worship, so that he takes his seat in the temple of God, proclaiming himself to be God.

According to the Bible, Jesus' second coming will be a public, unmistakable, and miraculous event that happens quickly. Verses emphasize its visible and dramatic nature, ruling out any secret or hidden arrival.

Public and unmistakable

Scriptures describe Jesus' return as a visible event that everyone will witness. Revelation 1:7 states "every eye will see him." Matthew 24:27 compares his coming to lightning that is seen "from the east and flashes as far as the west," indicating it will be universally apparent. Matthew 24:30 adds that people will "see the Son of Man coming on the clouds of heaven with power and great glory." Acts 1:11 confirms that he will return in the same visible manner in which he ascended into heaven.

Miraculous

The Bible also portrays this event as miraculous. 1 Thessalonians 4:16–17 describes the Lord descending from heaven with a command, an archangel's voice, and God's trumpet, leading to the resurrection of the dead in Christ and believers being "caught up together with them in the clouds to meet the Lord in the air." Second Thessalonians 1:7–10 depicts Jesus' revelation from heaven with angels and "flaming fire," demonstrating power and glory. Revelation 19:11–16 paints a picture of Jesus returning as "KING OF KINGS AND LORD OF LORDS" with the armies of heaven following him.

Quickly (or suddenly)

Several verses indicate the suddenness of Jesus' return. Revelation 22:12 and 22:20 quote Jesus saying, "I am coming soon." Second Peter 3:10 states, the Day of the Lord "will come like a thief in the night." Matthew 24:44 advises readiness because the "Son of Man is coming at an hour you do not expect," highlighting the unexpected nature of the timing.

THE FINAL PROOF

When read together, the prophets speak with one voice. The gathering of Israel is eschatological. It is Christ-centered. It is inseparable from repentance, resurrection, and the reign of the Messiah.

Partial returns: Babylonian, post-Roman, modern—may serve as shadows. They do not fulfill the substance. The prophets do not foresee a secular state stabilized by human resolve, but a sanctified kingdom transformed by divine presence.

The true gathering will be unmistakable.

The Spirit will be poured out.

The nations will acknowledge the Lord.

Death itself will be swallowed up.

Until that day, the proof remains future—written, promised, and sure.

The Voice of the Shepherd

> "My sheep hear My voice, and I know them, and they follow Me… and there shall be one flock and one Shepherd." (John 10:27)

The prophets, the apostles, and the Lord Himself speak as one. The final restoration is not the triumph of nationalism, but of grace. When the Shepherd calls, every scattered sheep—Jew and Gentile alike—will answer.

That day will be the proof beyond dispute: the covenant completed, the word fulfilled, and the kingdoms of this world become the kingdom of our Lord and of His Christ.

The prophetic testimony, taken as a whole, presents a coherent and demanding vision of restoration. Modern claims must therefore be measured—not dismissed, but tested—against that vision. It is this comparison that now lies before us.

Ch. 12: Modern Claims Measured Against Prophecy

I f the prophets provide the pattern, then history provides the test. Claims about Israel's modern restoration rise and fall on a single question: *Do present realities correspond to the prophetic conditions?* The issue is not whether something remarkable has occurred in modern Jewish history—few would deny that. The issue is whether those events constitute the fulfillment the prophets describe, or whether they represent something preliminary, partial, or altogether different.

This chapter does not deny history. It interrogates interpretation.

The Emergence of Modern Claims

The modern return of Jews to the land of Israel, culminating in the establishment of the State of Israel in 1948, has been widely hailed—especially within evangelical Christianity—as the long-awaited fulfillment of biblical prophecy.

Popular teaching often treats this event as self-authenticating proof:

The prophets spoke of return;

Jews have returned;

Therefore, prophecy is fulfilled.

Yet the prophets never offered return in isolation. They offered a *package*—a covenantal sequence involving repentance, divine intervention, messianic rule, spiritual renewal, and lasting peace. The burden of proof lies not in demonstrating similarity, but in demonstrating correspondence.

POLITICAL RESTORATION VS. PROPHETIC RESTORATION

Modern Israel is a political state recognized by international bodies such as the United Nations. It possesses borders, an army, diplomatic relations, and internal political divisions. These are the marks of nationhood, not the marks of prophetic fulfillment.

By contrast, the prophets speak of a restoration accomplished *by God Himself*, not negotiated through diplomacy or secured through military defense. The regathering they envision occurs at a moment of divine intervention so decisive that resistance collapses and recognition follows.

Prophetic restoration is not a fragile peace. It is final.

The Absence of National Repentance

One of the most consistent prophetic prerequisites for restoration is repentance—national, moral, and spiritual. Moses, Jeremiah, Ezekiel, Hosea, Joel, and Zechariah all place repentance before or alongside regathering. **Israel returns *to the Lord*, not merely to territory**.

Modern Israel, by contrast, is religiously pluralistic and largely secular. Its founding ideology was explicitly non-messianic, and in many cases overtly anti-religious. While religious Jews live within the state, the state itself does not represent covenant repentance, nor does it claim to.

This does not render modern Israel illegitimate as a nation. It renders it insufficient as prophetic fulfillment.

Messiah Still Unrecognized

The prophets repeatedly link Israel's restoration to the reign or recognition of the Messiah—described variously as the Branch, David the King, the Servant, or the Lord Himself. Zechariah is explicit: Israel's repentance is triggered by seeing the One she pierced. No such recognition has occurred. Modern Israel does not confess Jesus as Messiah, nor does it claim to live under messianic rule. The absence of this defining feature alone places modern claims outside the prophetic horizon.

Any fulfillment without the King present is, by definition, incomplete.

Peace That Has Not Come

Isaiah and Micah envision an age in which war ceases, weapons are repurposed, and the nations learn peace from Zion. Ezekiel speaks of secure dwelling without fear. Amos promises a planting never again uprooted. Modern Israel exists in a state of chronic insecurity, surrounded by hostility, dependent on force, and marked by repeated conflict. To call this the age of prophetic peace requires redefining peace beyond recognition.

The prophets did not speak of survival. They spoke of transformation.

The "Already" without the "Not Yet"

Some theologians attempt to resolve these tensions by appealing to partial fulfillment. According to this view, modern Israel fulfills the physical aspects of prophecy, while spiritual fulfillment awaits a later stage.

Yet the prophets themselves resist such division. Physical regathering, spiritual renewal, and messianic reign are consistently intertwined. When Ezekiel separates stages, it is only to show sequence—not independence. Physical restoration without spiritual resurrection is never presented as fulfillment.

Partial shadows are acknowledged in Scripture; final fulfillment is not confused with shadows.

THE DANGER OF PROPHETIC INFLATION

When modern political events are treated as prophetic certainties, Scripture becomes reactive rather than authoritative. Current events begin to dictate interpretation instead of interpretation governing how events are assessed.

This inversion carries theological risk. It pressures readers to defend actions, policies, or conflicts as divinely sanctioned simply because they involve Israel. The prophets never granted such immunity. On the contrary, they judged Israel more severely than the nations precisely because of covenant responsibility.

To defend everything Israel does in the name of prophecy is not biblical faithfulness. It is prophetic distortion.

Covenant Faithfulness without Premature Fulfillment

Acknowledging that modern Israel does not fulfill prophecy does not require denying God's faithfulness to Israel. The endurance of the Jewish people, their survival against overwhelming odds and their continued presence in the land may indeed testify to divine preservation.

Preservation, however, is not consummation.

The prophets anticipate a moment when preservation gives way to resurrection, when survival gives way to glory, and when history gives way to renewal.

A Measured Conclusion

Measured against the prophetic standard, modern claims fall short—not because the prophets failed, but because their horizon has not yet arrived. The decisive markers remain absent:

- National repentance has not occurred.
- The Messiah is not acknowledged.
- The Spirit has not been poured out universally.
- Peace has not been established.
- Resurrection has not taken place.

Until these conditions converge, the prophetic gathering remains future.

Preparing for the Final Question

If modern Israel is not the fulfillment, then what role— if any—does it play in God's unfolding purposes? Is it a sign, a stage, a shadow, or simply a historical reality awaiting interpretation? These questions lead naturally to the final inquiry of this book: *What, then, should believers conclude—and how should they speak responsibly about Israel today?*

It is to that concluding task that we now turn.

Ch. 13: What Then Shall We Say?

COVENANT, HOPE, AND FAITHFULNESS IN THE PRESENT AGE

Every serious theological inquiry eventually arrives at a point where evidence has been weighed, texts examined, and conclusions drawn—yet questions remain. Not questions of uncertainty, but questions of posture. *How, then, should we live? How should we speak? How should we hope?*

This book has argued that Israel remains central to the biblical story, that the covenant has not been revoked, and that the prophets speak with remarkable clarity about the nature and timing of Israel's restoration. It has also argued that modern claims of fulfillment, however sincere, do not meet the prophetic standard. The gathering promised by Scripture is eschatological, messianic, and transformative in ways history has not yet displayed.

What follows, then, is not a call to speculation, but to faithfulness.

Holding Together What Scripture Refuses to Separate

One of the great temptations in theology is simplification. Faced with complexity, we reduce; faced with tension, we resolve prematurely.

Yet Scripture itself resists this impulse. It holds together truths that appear, at first glance, to pull in opposite directions.

Israel is chosen—and Israel is judged.

The covenant is irrevocable—and participation in it is morally serious.

The promises are sure—and their fulfillment is future.

The Church is grafted in—and Israel is not cast aside.

To affirm one at the expense of the others is not clarity; it is distortion. The biblical vision is richer, more demanding, and ultimately more hopeful than our systems often allow.

Israel without Idolatry, the Church without Arrogance

This study has sought to avoid two equal and opposite errors.

The first is **national idolatry**—the tendency to treat modern Israel as above biblical critique, as though covenant election guarantees divine endorsement of every political action. The prophets never permitted such reasoning. Israel's chosenness intensified responsibility; it did not cancel accountability.

The second error is **ecclesial arrogance**—the assumption that the Church has fully replaced Israel in God's purposes, rendering the Jewish people theologically irrelevant except as historical background. This posture ignores the plain teaching of Scripture and flattens the covenant story into abstraction. Faithfulness requires resisting both temptations.

THE MEANING OF WAITING

If the prophetic gathering lies in the future, then the present age is, by definition, an age of waiting. But biblical waiting is not passivity. It is moral readiness, spiritual attentiveness, and covenant fidelity in the absence of sight.

Israel waits for recognition of her Messiah.

The Church waits for His return.

Creation itself waits for renewal.

This shared posture is not accidental. It binds together Jew and Gentile under a single hope without erasing distinction. The final restoration will not belong to one people at the expense of another, but will reveal the wisdom of God in uniting all things in Christ.

177

Reading History without Forcing It

History matters. Events matter. The survival of the Jewish people matters. The reemergence of Israel as a nation matters. But history must be interpreted *through* Scripture, not Scripture retrofitted to history.

When current events are elevated to prophetic certainty, theology becomes reactive. When Scripture governs interpretation, history is allowed to speak without being forced to say more than it does.

The prophets themselves model this restraint. They speak with confidence about the end while remaining patient within the present. They recognize shadows without mistaking them for substance.

Hope without Haste

Christian hope is not fragile, and it does not require constant validation through headlines. The future promised by God does not advance by human urgency or ideological pressure. It arrives at the appointed time.

The danger of haste is not merely error, but disappointment. When expectations are set too low—when prophecy is declared fulfilled too soon—the inevitable gaps between promise and reality lead either to disillusionment or to ever more strained reinterpretations.

The prophets offer a better path: confidence without presumption, expectation without manipulation.

The Final Shape of the Story

When the Scriptures speak of the end, they do so with remarkable consistency. Israel is restored. The Messiah reigns. The nations are gathered. Justice is established. Death is defeated. Creation is renewed.

This is not the triumph of one ethnicity or institution. It is the unveiling of God's faithfulness across time. Israel's story does not end in obsolescence, and the Church's story does not end in isolation. Both find their meaning in the same consummation.

Until that day, neither may claim finality.

A CALL TO FAITHFUL SPEECH

Perhaps the most practical outcome of this study is not a chart or a timeline, but a manner of speaking.

How Christians talk about Israel reveals how they read Scripture, how they understand covenant, and how they perceive God's faithfulness.

Faithful speech avoids exaggeration. Faithful speech resists fear-driven prophecy. Faithful speech honors Israel without baptizing politics. Faithful speech affirms the Church without erasing Israel.

Above all, faithful speech keeps its eyes fixed on Christ—the center toward which all covenant and prophecy move.

THE PROOF THAT REMAINS

The proof about Israel is not finally found in borders, ballots, or battles. It is found in the unwavering consistency of God's word across millennia. What He promised, He will do. What He has begun, He will complete.

The gathering remains future.

The kingdom remains coming.

The covenant remains sure.

And until the day when the Shepherd gathers every scattered sheep and reigns in undisputed righteousness, the proper response is neither denial nor declaration—but trust.

> "He who scattered Israel will gather him,
> and keep him as a shepherd does his flock."

That promise has not failed.

It has not yet finished.

Bibliography

Alliance Israélite Universelle. Archival materials referenced in discussions of nineteenth-century Jewish settlement initiatives in Palestine.

Bauer, Bruno. *Die Judenfrage*. Braunschweig: F. Vieweg, 1843.

Chernilo, Daniel. "The Rise and Rise of the 'Israel Question.'" In *The New Jewish Question: Global Modernity and the State of Israel*. New York: Routledge, 2024.

Hess, Moses. *Rome and Jerusalem: The Last National Question*. Leipzig: Eduard Mendelssohn, 1862.

Herzl, Theodor. *Der Judenstaat*. Vienna: M. Brettauer, 1896.

Kalischer, Zvi Hirsch. *Derishat Tsiyon*. 1862.

League of Nations. *Mandate for Palestine*. 1922.

Lindsey, Hal. *The Late Great Planet Earth*. Grand Rapids: Zondervan, 1970; *The 1980s: Countdown to Armageddon*. New York: Bantam, 1980.

MERIP Reports. "Israel and the Jewish Question." No. 131 (March 1985).

Said, Edward W. "Question of Palestine." UNISPAL Archives.

Steele, Philip Earl. "Rabbi Kalischer from Toruń – the Father of Religious Zionism." *Jewish Heritage Europe*, December 20, 2021.

United Nations. *Resolution 181 (II): Future Government of Palestine*. 1947.

Biography

C. W. Steinle is a distinguished author, teacher, and commentator recognized for his contributions to biblical theology, prophecy, and the intersection of faith and science. With a professional background as a Certified Public Accountant (CPA), Steinle brings analytical rigor to theological studies, combining research precision with pastoral insight. His bibliography spans more than twenty-five titles, including *The Rise of Western Lawlessness*—a study of cultural and ideological shifts in modern society— and *Reclaiming the Rapture*, co-authored with Dr. Douglas Hamp, which critically examines dispensationalist traditions in eschatology. Steinle's scholarship has been widely cited, with over 2,000 references on Academia.edu, and he frequently contributes to Christian media as a guest commentator and teacher.

Extensively traveled, Steinle has taught on site in Israel, Philippi, Thessaloniki, Corinth, Athens, Sinai, and Egypt, bringing historical and geographical depth to his biblical expositions.